Renovating with a Contractor

Renovating with a Contractor

Kevin Brenner and Kate Kelly

Taylor Publishing Company
Dallas, Texas

The illustrations on the following pages are by Francis D.K. Ching and are reprinted with permission by Van Nostrand Reinhold: 123, 125, 126, 128, 129, 130, 140, 141, 142, 148, 149, 150, 154, and 155.

Published by Taylor Publishing Company
1550 West Mockingbird Lane
Dallas, Texas 75235

Designed by Hespenheide Design

Library of Congress Cataloging-in-Publication Data

Brenner, Kevin.
        Renovating with a contractor: the complete home-
owner's guide to updating or adding on to your house
using a home contractor / by Kevin Brenner and Kate
Kelly.
        p.   cm.
        ISBN 0-87833-904-3
        1. Dwellings—Remodeling.   2. Contracting out.
I. Kelly, Kate, 1950–   II. Title.
TH4816.B73.   1996   95-44167
643' .7'068—dc20   CIP

Printed in the United States of America
10 9 8 7 6 5 4 3 2 1

In loving memory of my father, Dr. Norman Brenner, who shared with me his love of life and enthusiasm for building things that continue to guide me even today; and to my wife, Jill, and our three children, Zachary, Kate, and Ari, who I love even though I'm never home.

—K.S.B.

To Sheryl Shaker, who first introduced me to the concept of home remodeling as a wonderful adventure. With her advice and creative thinking, our household projects have always exceeded our dreams.

—K.K.

Contents

► Introduction

The best advice anyone can give you about undertaking home renovation is to plan, prepare, and use a pro.

If you're like most people, your home is your single largest financial investment, and if home improvements are part of your future, you want to do them right—both for your own peace of mind and for eventually being able to recoup, if not increase, your investment.

The problem is that home remodeling is, at best, unsettling. At worst, it can be a disaster, financially and emotionally. Many people plunge into it with little more than a vague vision of what they want and no idea of what's involved. As a result, the project goes badly—costing more, taking longer, and creating much more family tension than anyone had anticipated.

Like anything else, knowledge of a subject can ease the process, and that's the reason for this book. We want to help you understand what you're undertaking—planning the project, prioritizing what to do now and what must wait, hiring a good contractor, and preparing for something that will ultimately result in a positive change. We want to show you how to maneuver intelligently through the remodeling process.

By virtue of having purchased this book, you must already be convinced of the wisdom of relying on a professional contractor (and we'll advise you on selecting a good one). You've made a smart decision. You can shift a huge burden off your shoulders by letting a home contractor manage the job. Let someone else worry about ordering the right amount of lumber at the best price (and getting it delivered on time), and let someone else take responsibility for getting the subfloor of the bathroom replaced unexpectedly before the new tile is laid. You'll still have plenty to do functioning as overall project administrator, a job you'll learn how to do well in the pages of this book.

What expertise do we bring to this book? We're people who have been there—one of us from each side of the homeowner-contractor fence. I'm a writer and homeowner who has lived through several home renovation projects, ranging from structural changes in an apartment, new baths in my current home, and a major addition in between. A husband, three children, and a dog have all participated in the process. Some of my children's most vivid memories concern home renovation, like "the day Jimmy The Carpenter was there, and there was this beeping and the fire engines came." There's nothing like instant entertainment in your own home! (I'll tell you how to avoid being thus amused.)

Before construction began, I tried to read what I could about remodeling, and I was astonished to find that there was very little in print that would help me become knowledgeable about the process. Although I found a few books that offered advice on how to hire a contractor, they dropped me cold after that. No book continued past where most families feel the story begins—the day the demolition team arrives to start chopping out what's going to be replaced!

My assignment is to provide the homeowner's viewpoint as we walk you through the process. From me, you'll hear how important it is to plan your remodeling in careful detail. I'll also offer advice on how to minimize dust and disruption, how to be realistic in your expectations of both the project and the experience, how to get the most out of the workers who are entering your home, and which of the "standard practices" of remodeling are worth fighting about.

You'll hear, too, directly from a contractor, Kevin Brenner, who will provide technical information and insight as to why they do what they do. Kevin is a home contractor and president of his own remodeling company—Brenner Builders of New Rochelle, New York. He learned about home remodeling as he grew up. His father, a doctor, loved doing projects around the home, and together he and Kevin tackled everything from building a deck to remodeling a vacation home. Kevin helped pay his way through college and medical school by working for various construction companies, and while still in school he started his own business. By the time he graduated, he realized he preferred to continue doing the construction work he loved instead of practicing medicine.

Today, twelve years later, Brenner Builders undertakes projects ranging from bathroom renovations to new home construction, and the company keeps several crews working at all times. Clients appreciate Kevin's enthusiasm for the work, his dedication to home contracting as a profession, and his active pursuit of staying current in the field. His wife, Jill, just laughs when his stack of vacation reading is topped off with *The Journal of Light Construction*.

No doubt about it, Kevin knows houses inside and out. On a job, he'll climb into any attic and inch along any crawl space he has to. He started out doing the work himself, which makes him well prepared to tell you what's going on, how it can be done most efficiently, and what you can do to help the contractor stay on time and within budget. If you follow his advice, you'll get better value from the dollars you invest in any construction project, large or small.

Five years ago Kevin was the contractor we selected to build an addition on our home. Brenner Builders has been back to renovate and repair in between, and during that time Kevin began talking about the book he wished his clients could have. He frequently gets calls from people who have no idea what they want, only that they want "a bigger kitchen" or "a new bathroom." He wanted them to have this book to read to help them think through what they have in mind, to let them know exactly what they should do to prepare, and what they should expect as the work progresses.

The result is *Renovating with a Contractor*. It is written for you, the homeowner, to take you step-by-step through all phases of adding to or updating a home using a professional remodeler. We maintain that a homeowner who understands the remodeling process, who hires the contractor carefully, and who knows how to cope with the inevitable disruptions caused by even a small project will be spared much of the unpleasantness people often go through in renovating their homes. Throughout this book, we also offer advice on how to control expenses and avoid expensive delays and costly problems during the various stages of home remodeling. (Kevin's got a long list of suggestions for homeowners that can really speed the process along!)

There is something really exciting about a crew arriving at your house to make your dreams come true. We can't guarantee that every day will be a dust-free delight, but we can assure you that we'll give you the information you need to help see that the project goes as smoothly as possible. And, if you're really fortunate, you'll enjoy the people you've hired to do the work. As your project draws to a close, you'll be delighted to do a cleanup that stays that way, but you might even feel a twinge of regret to see the crew move on to their next job.

In the end, you'll have what you've been dreaming of—a new kitchen, a bedroom for the baby, a family room and screened porch, an up-to-date bathroom, whatever change was important to you and that makes your home life easier and more comfortable. At that point, you can put our book on a shelf until your next undertaking. Or when the doorbell rings and a neighbor is asking about the work you've had done, maybe you'll say, "Hold on a minute. Have I got the book for you!"

Good luck. It's an exciting process, and we're here to take you through it from beginning to end.

Chapter 1

To Remodel or Not to Remodel?

Here are some of the reasons people remodel their homes. Do any of them sound familiar?

"We bought an older house that was a great size for our family, but the kitchen was outdated and in poor condition. With four children we needed a modern kitchen that made meal-making and cleanup easy."

"I started my own business and wanted a separate space for a home office."

"When we first moved to this area, we could only afford a smaller home. Then we had children and needed the space. Because we liked the neighborhood and were really attached to some of the special qualities of our house, we decided to add on."

"We'd intended to move to a larger home, but we wanted to keep the children in the same school they had been attending, and when we looked at what we would have to pay for a larger home in our area, it made financial sense to improve the home we were in."

"We bought a house that had been neglected for years, and we had to do some work before we moved in."

"Our home is a never-ending project. We believe that it's important to update everything from the water heater to the paint job, so we do what-ever seems most pressing every couple of years."

Or perhaps you're facing the same dilemma that many homeowners face: "Should I search for a new home that has what I'm looking for, or should I remodel the one I already own?"

There are many good reasons for remodeling. Our homes are impor-tant to us, and we look to them to fill a wide range of needs, far beyond a basic desire to have a warm and inviting place to eat and sleep.

With today's lifestyles, space and more space is a constant issue. In addition, some homeowners are looking for a variety of specialized items. They are creating homes with oversized kitchens for gourmet cooking, media rooms to accommodate the latest in viewing and listening materials, computer stations for the kids and themselves, garages that will hold additional vehicles as well as the objects of various hobbies, and beautiful porches and decks. Although most people don't have all of these amenities, those who invest in a new home or opt to remodel are looking to have one or two of these special features in the dream home they create.

Regardless of the reasons for contemplating remodeling, homeowners share common worries. Lack of understanding the process, apprehension over cost, dread at the thought of living through a renovation, and worry over losing money in a home improvement that doesn't go well are all perfectly valid concerns that can be allayed if you do your homework along the way.

Let's start with the first puzzlement: How do you get from your current home to that dream home—or at least a home with enough space?

Most people have no idea. They go to a contractor or make an appointment with an architect and say they want "more space" or "a better bathroom (we don't want pink tiles)" or a "bigger kitchen." Anything that results from such vague direction is destined to cost more than you ever intended, and it will be the contractor's or the architect's kitchen or bathroom, not yours, because you've skipped some important steps: those that determine what you really want and need.

Getting Started

First, you and your spouse should go through the following process. (These steps are important for anyone considering home renovation, though a few of the questions are specifically to help those who are also considering the possibility of a move.) Answer the questions thoughtfully, and then allow a few days for adding to and rethinking your answers.

1. What are the reasons you are considering remodeling your house (or possibly buying a new one)? Do you need more space? Have your space needs changed because the children have grown up and moved out? Is your lifestyle changing (are you going back to work? starting a home business?, etc.)?
2. On three separate pieces of paper answer the following questions:
   - What are the elements you particularly like about your current home?
   - If you stay in your current home, what is its major drawback? What would you change so that it will better meet your needs?

- If you move, what specific qualities would a new home have to have to make it worth your while? (This list should include items from both of the above lists. If you already have a new kitchen you love, you might not want to lose it if you move.)
3. Describe elements of your lifestyle that affect the way you use your home.
   - Are you home a great deal?
   - Do you entertain often?
   - Is your home a hangout for your kids and their friends?
   - Does anyone in the family work out of a home office?
   - In what rooms does the family spend the most time?
4. Are you satisfied with your neighborhood? If not, what would you like to have in a new neighborhood?
5. Do you have rigid time constraints for any household changes? (A new baby can be shuffled from room to room for awhile. If the space is being added for an elderly parent who is moving in with you, it would be much better to have the new space ready before she moves in.)
6. Temperamentally do you think you will be relatively comfortable with the planning, work, and disruption that come with remodeling? (Renovating is a big project.)

Buy a "Home Renovation" Notebook

If you're considering undertaking a household project, it's vital that you be organized in thought as well as in action. You'll soon realize that a "small addition" and a "simple bathroom" involve an amazing number of details.

To organize this information (and this is just the beginning of the information-gathering process), buy these materials:

- a standard-size loose-leaf binder
- lined loose-leaf paper
- a set of subject dividers with pockets. (The pockets will provide a place to put the miscellaneous papers and brochures you'll acquire throughout the process.)

The first items to put in your notebook are the results of your answers to the above. These papers will serve as helpful personal checklists.

Resolving the Move or Improve Issue

Unless you already know that remodeling is for you, the next thing you owe yourself is a home search.

From the lists created in number 2 above, create a "home require-ments" list for your real estate agent. (To select a helpful Realtor, get referrals from friends.) This list will give all of you a working document that details what you want to gain and what you're not willing to give up if you move. And don't worry about approaching a Realtor on a "maybe I'll move and maybe I won't" basis. That's part of their business. They know buying a new home is a tremendous investment, and part of their job is helping people explore the market. Sometimes the return on time spent with a client is a big sale; other times it's a positive referral to a new client. (And after all, if they find the perfect home for you at the right price, you will buy it.)

To house hunt, of course, you're going to need to establish a price range. For most people, this will depend heavily upon the money your current home will bring. To get an estimate of what your home might sell for in today's market, ask your Realtor to prepare a market analysis of your home. By doing so, you will get a relatively accurate estimate. This figure, combined with the additional amount (in the form of sav-ings or a loan) you expect to invest in your home, will give you an idea of your house-hunting price range. When you consider these costs, remember to factor in attendant costs: commissions paid to the Realtor, moving expenses, etc.

Let's suppose your search is fruitful. If the house of your dreams is out there, ready-built, and on the market, you might as well just move in and enjoy it! (Wrap this book up and present it to a friend who's think-ing of renovating, or put it on a shelf in your new home and use it when you decide that something in your new home needs to be updated.)

But even if you don't find the perfect house, your hunt will have been beneficial. You will have learned about home design by seeing other houses and have a better understanding of the market and the ele-ments of a home people place special value on. Remember, if you see qualities you'd like to incorporate in your renovation, write them down in your notebook.

Remodeling requires a 100% commitment, so it's important that you don't later muse, "Maybe I really should have moved . . ."

It makes sense to renovate when you:

- want to add more space but can't afford a new home or don't find one that meets your needs,
- want to make your home more functional,
- want to add character to a basic home, or
- want to increase the pleasure you get from your home.

Affordability

What will you have to spend to accomplish what you want? Ah, the most difficult question.

It would be nice to be able to walk into The Great Remodeling Store and price the job the way we shop for shoes: "Kitchen with Corian Counters: $30,000; No Frills Bathroom Addition: $12,000."

Unfortunately, at this stage, it's impossible to know what your home renovation will really cost. There are still too many decisions to be made.

Neighbors and friends who have recently remodeled will give you some idea of costs, and area architects or designers can give you an average square-foot price. There is also a book, *The Means Building Construction Cost Data,* that describes typical home-improvement costs with tables that are set up so that you can find your costs by zip code. Ask for it at your library.

Another possibility is doing a rough sketch of what you have in mind (or write it down in list form) and stop by a remodeling supply store. The staff there would be able to give you a range of prices that correspond to the prices of similar projects being done in your home. Although you're a long way from an ultimate price tag, having a general idea of where costs are going may be of some comfort. Like everything else, these prices are dependent on the choices you make.

Where Will the Money Come from?

A recent survey conducted by the National Association of Home Builders' Remodeler's Council found that 52% of homeowners paid for their home improvements out of savings, 27% initiated equity loans, 18% used other loans, and 5% depended upon liquidation of assets or proceeds from the sale of a previous home.

This is a good time to begin to examine what might work for you.

Home Equity Loan

For renovations of more than $10,000, loans that permit you to borrow against the value you've built up in your home offer certain advantages. With a home equity loan, if your home's current market value is $225,000 and you owe $125,000 on the balance of the mortgage, you have $100,000 worth of equity. Banks will generally lend you up to 75%–80% of this amount.

Home equity loans fall into two separate categories: a straight loan or a line of credit. If you prefer to receive a check for the entire amount and make a steady set of payments over time, then yours will be a staight loan. Straight loans provide you with a lump sum that you pay back via a steady set of payments over time. They are recommended for projects of short duration.

A home equity line of credit lets the homeowner draw the money as needed. This can be a less expensive way to borrow money because you take it out only when you need it, and interest accrues only on what you draw out. A line of credit is preferred when the renovation is stretched out over a long period and payments to the contractor are erratic.

Installment Loans

Installment loans can be secured or unsecured. **Home improvement loans** are secured, and the interest is tax deductible. The payback is generally five to seven years, so the monthly payment is smaller because it's spread over several years.

A **personal loan** is the unsecured version of an installment loan. These rely solely on your income and credit history. There is no stipulation as to what the money is to be used for, but generally these carry higher interest rates and terms are shorter—typically one to three years, making the monthly payment relatively high.

If your housing meets certain guidelines or your income falls in a certain range (middle class may still qualify), you might qualify for a **Title I loan**. These enable some banks to offer 15-year home-improvement loans with a reduced monthly payment. (See the resource section at the back of the book for information on *The Consumer's Guide to Home Repair Grants and Subsidized Loans*.)

Refinancing Your Mortgage

Most banks will let you mortgage up to 65%–75% of your home, so if your home has increased in value you can get more money even after you've paid off your original mortgage. This is a longer term option that offers the advantage of lower payments. However, some families do not want to commit to a long-term obligation if they have major expenses such as college looming on the horizon. In addition, up-front costs of refinancing are higher than borrowing against your equity.

Contractor-Provided Loans

Some of the larger home remodeling firms are prepared to lend homeowners money for the work. Contractor-provided loans should only be considered after you have shopped around and know that it is competitive with other loans available in the marketplace.

Am I Making a Wise Investment?

In all likelihood, your home is the single largest investment you have. It's the only one you have much control over, so if you invest wisely and judiciously in home improvement, chances are good that your investment will hold up over time.

"So if I invest $25,000 in a new kitchen renovation, can I tack $25,000 on to the price of my home?" you might ask. Not exactly. (If you plan to sell soon, paint—don't renovate. Potential buyers may not like your ideas, and there's no sense in going through the headache of a renovation if you're not going to be there to appreciate it.)

What you will find is that a home that is neglected and not kept up-to-date will decrease in value, while the home that has been cared for and improved will hold its value. So will you get every dollar back that you ever spent on home improvements? Probably not. What you will get is a faster sale and a better price than comparable homes in your market.

Homeowners often worry about overimproving, and rightly so. In most neighborhoods, real estate agents say that improvements are limited by a 30% rule. They increase the value of a home by only 30% over the price of the cheapest home. Ideally, a renovation should bring you from one part of the value range in your neighborhood up to another—not beyond.

"Don't overimprove" is wise advice, but you also have to take into account quality of life. An exercise room in your basement may hold no value to the next homeowner, but if it's something you use every day then it is something that is right for you. (Over time the investment may cost less, for example, than the investment in an annual membership at a gym.) But most importantly, you will have improved the quality of your own lifestyle in the process. No one can put a dollar value on that.

What's Hot, What's Not

As you discuss exactly what your renovation will involve, it may help to know about the categories of various remodeling projects and whether or not they enhance value. The first three categories best summarize the most popular reasons for remodeling. However, the latter two can be beneficial as well. Most projects span a couple of categories.

Space additions. These usually involve building out from the footprint of the house. However, sometimes these projects are a "reclaiming" of existing space, perhaps finishing off a basement or attic or converting a garage into liveable space. A well-done space addition will generally add value; one that is tacked on or done poorly can actually hurt the value of a basic home.

General remodeling with changes to the floor plan. This type of remodeling is often complex because it involves reconfiguring existing space. These projects add value if done well but drop value if done badly. Generally the most successful ones, in terms of resale, are ones where what is being added is something that other homes in the area have. For example, an expanded kitchen made with top quality materials and appliances is a definite benefit in a neighborhood of luxury homes.

Luxury additions. These are amenities that are added for the comfort of today's owners and might include a fireplace, skylight, pool, central air conditioning, security systems, deck, hot tub, darkroom, tennis court, greenhouse, central vacuuming, or central audio systems. With the exception of a fireplace or skylight, these items are so personal that it's frequently difficult to get back your investment. However, certain home remodeling decisions are made for quality-of-life enhancement, so if you have the money there's no reason not to do them.

Cosmetic face lifts. These are projects that improve the appearance of a room or the exterior of the home but do not require major demolition in order to be accomplished. Painting, landscaping, installing a new floor, adding new appliances or fixtures, or restoring or refinishing cabinetry are the types of projects that fall into this category. Putting down a new floor or repainting a room can freshen a room immeasurably, and, in combination with a larger remodeling project, a cosmetic face lift can be used to save money. You might want to update your kitchen and the appliances but can save and repaint the old kitchen cabinets that give the room character.

System upgrades. These projects improve the functional quality of the home. They don't necessarily show, but they generally provide a good short-term return on the investment. Projects in this category include replacing or improving the electrical, plumbing, heating, and cooling systems, or replacing windows and doors, roof, and weather stripping. (If you're married, you'll likely find that this is one type of home remodeling on which couples frequently disagree. My husband loves attic fans, new wiring, and basement upkeep; I have little interest in opening the door to an electrician unless he's carrying a new light fixture under his arm. I prefer fresh paint, new floors, and moving walls around.)

Remodeling magazine produces a "Cost vs. Value Report" that records the cost and the payback of specific home remodeling projects in various parts of the country. (See the resource section for more information.) The following table cites a few examples, along with their national averages.

If you are still concerned about what remodeling will do to the value of your home, talk to an expert. This time you need something more specific than a general assessment of market value from your Realtor. For a more accurate evaluation, call an appraiser (available through most real estate firms). For $150 to $300, they will research prices of homes in your area and then check on sales of homes with amenities similar to yours. When you talk to them about assessing your home, tell them you're considering remodeling and ask for an assessment of what

Major Kitchen Remodeling:
Cost: $17,170   Resale Value: $16,270   Investment Recouped: 95%

Minor Kitchen Remodeling:
Cost: $5,835   Resale Value: $6,042   Investment Recouped: 104%

Bathroom Remodeling:
Cost: $6,443   Resale Value: $5,292   Investment Recouped: 82%

Family Room Addition:
Cost: $27,221   Resale Value: $24,019   Investment Recouped: 88%

Two-story Addition:
Cost: $50,596   Resale Value: $42,438   Investment Recouped: 84%

it will do to the value of your home. (They may need plans in order to perform this step.) After getting this information, you will feel more comfortable with deciding how to proceed.

Remember, too, that ultimately you will realize some financial bene-fits from tax breaks. Improvements that extend the life of your house, increase its value, or adapt it for another use will be deductible on resale. Save your receipts, records, and blueprints as proof of what you've done.

Idea Gathering

In the process of house hunting, you've likely gotten some ideas for amenities you might like in your own home, and these should be writ-ten down in your notebook so that you can consider them at the appro-priate time. Your next step is more research.

Now the homes you need to visit are those in which remodeling or ren-ovation has taken place. Call friends and ask to see their renovated homes. While touring for general ideas, listen for two pieces of information:

1. What do they like about their renovation and what do they wish they had done differently? (You may think the "high hat" lighting in the kitchen looks wonderful; they may have criticisms of it.)
2. What were some of the costs? Friends may not want to discuss specifics, but they probably will give you a ballpark range for what their bids on a new kitchen or bath were. Knowing these general prices is vital to helping you estimate what you will be able to do and at what cost. Keep in mind that there will still be variations. Like anything else, a wide variety of variables go into pricing home

construction—how many years ago the construction took place, how busy the contractor is, what kind of condition the original house is in, whether or not there were "in-wall" surprises. All make a difference in what you will pay. Also, take note of whether the result was a "no frills" job or one using top-quality materials.

Be creative as you research. One family spotted a house in their neighborhood with a new addition similar to what they hoped to do. By making a few phone calls they were able to find someone who knew the family so that they could get a tour. They met the people, saw the home, and ultimately used the same architect for the project.

Stop by showrooms. If you're going to redo a bathroom, there's no time like now to begin looking at what is available in fixtures and hardware. The more you know about an area, the easier it will be to renovate. (Remember to make note of good ideas and take copies of brochures; file them in your notebook so that you'll have them when you need them later on.)

In addition to touring homes and visiting showrooms, start reading magazines. The traditional shelter magazines are good, but keep an eye out for the specialty magazines that focus on kitchens and baths. Tear out articles and pictures that appeal to you (even if all you like in the picture is a bench, pull the picture and put it in your notebook). This collection of "what I like" will give your designer or architect a head start in developing ideas that appeal to you.

As you proceed, you'll begin to gather names of designers, architects, and contractors. Write those down. Finding someone to help you shape your dream into a reality is an important step in this project.

Establish Goals

At this point, you've done enough research that you can begin to write down the specific goals of what you want to achieve. Create two columns: "What We MUST Have" and "What We'd LIKE to Have." These items should be combined with the original lists placed in your notebook so that you begin to develop a complete list of the home remodeling job you'd like to do.

Feasibility: Will Your Community Let You Do It?

If you've come this far, then you have a general idea of what you plan to do to your home. The final step in this early stage is to explore the project's feasibility. This is most easily accomplished by visiting the office of your local building department to check on local requirements. While there, you'll want answers to the following questions:

INSIDER'S TIP

Invest Time Now

We haven't even talked about calling a contractor, and yet if you've followed some or all of the advice so far, you've probably spent several weeks thinking about what we've talked about in this chapter. This process takes a long time! For anything bigger than a deck, families generally consider and plan for several months before making a change.

One architect says: "I tell my clients that a project is going to be a lot of fun and a lot of work, and they shouldn't get into it if they aren't prepared to devote the time."

Investing time in the beginning will also save time, money, and stress later on. It isn't as much fun as watching a carpenter build a new wall for your home office, but it's a lot more sensible. You can think through your goals and priorities before you start paying someone to help you. The better organized and the more focused you are before the process begins, the more smoothly the project will proceed, and the less you'll pay for it.

Time also provides clarity of thought. You'd be surprised at some of the realizations you'll come to only after letting a project simmer. One family moved into a new home knowing that they needed to add a downstairs powder room. They intended that the bathroom be built between the dining room and the den area where the family liked to watch TV. There were delays in getting contractor bids, so several months passed after the plans were drawn. As they sat in the den one night, the wife turned to the husband with the realization, "I don't want the bathroom right off this room. Everyone in the dining room will watch as people enter the bathroom, and anyone in the den will be disturbed by the flushing of the toilet."

Though they'd walked through the plans with the architect and had weighed the pros and cons of various locations, it took sitting in the quiet of the den one evening to realize exactly what it would be like to have the bathroom placed there.

The family incurred extra cost in having the plans changed slightly, but they were happy they were spared what they viewed as a big mistake.

- Will I need a permit?
- What are the back- and side-yard setbacks?
- Are there special requirements for fences or decks (if your project will involve them)?

Double the Time and Double the Money

Have you heard this remark from people when they are talking about home construction? All too often, it's true.

But that's why we've written this book. By asking that you make decisions and set specific goals before hiring your first worker, we'll help you avoid the problems with "double the time." And throughout the book, we'll offer advice to make the money side come out right, too. There are two areas where costs get out of line.

1. People hire an architect or planner who encourages them to talk about their entire wish list, without much thought to priorities. The planner then promises that virtually everything can be accomplished for whatever it was the family planned to spend. When bid out, the project comes in at three and four times cost. Helping your planner stay within your target figure is one of the most important goals of this book.
2. The second area where costs get out of line is on the "while-ya's." The homeowner realizes that carpenters are in the house, and all of a sudden that old back door

looks pretty bad. The next thing out of the homeowner's mouth is, "While you're here could you . . ." After a while, those while-ya's add up. That's why we've added a special chapter on them. Homeowners are correct in thinking that this is, indeed, the perfect time to get some projects taken care of. If you plan on those tasks ahead of time, then they can be a part of the initial budget estimate instead of an "add on." It will also save you money. Items that are part of the original estimate will generally be priced more reasonably than those that are tacked on once the job is underway.

It is reasonable to expect that your costs will probably run about 10% over your estimated figure. The unexpected can and does occur. For instance: once the walls are open in the bathroom, the contractor discovers that pipes, thought to be fine, ought to be replaced, or there may be water damage, or an entire community of termites may have been dining on your wood. . . . There will be unexpected expenses, but there are still ways to control costs.

If you will need a zoning variance, ask for advice from the staff on writing up your application. Sometimes there is specific wording that will set off alarms, and you don't want to start out on the wrong foot.

And if you're saying, "Who needs a permit? No one will know I'm switching a few things around in the bathroom," don't even think of it. The permit process protects you, and you'll be unable to proceed until you get the proper permissions and a proper certificate of occupancy. It's never pleasant to have to do this after the fact and under the stress of wanting to sell.

Homeowner Checklist

- Decide what your remodeling goals are.
- Buy a notebook to hold your ideas and the product information that you'll acquire.
- House hunt if you're still doubtful.
- Explore the different options available for financing the project.
- Consider the type of remodeling you might do and its effect on your housing value.
- Hire an appraiser if you're extremely concerned about what remodeling will do to value.
- Visit your local building department to explore the feasibility of your ideas.

Chapter 2

Choosing Your Team: Architects, Designers, and Other Specialists

One of the most common mistakes people make when adding on or renovating is failing to see the big picture. They'll tack a family room onto the back of their house without considering exterior appearance, traffic pattern, or furniture placement—all important elements of well-planned space. Or they'll redo the basement by putting up some Sheetrock, never realizing that with a little thought (and maybe some outside advice) there's a way to create a storage room, exercise room, and playroom at only slightly more cost than what they are already spending.

You may want an extra bedroom, a remodeled bathroom, or a home office, but do you really feel prepared to plan out all the electrical, engineering, plumbing, construction, and building details that will need to be a part of the project?

That's where architects and designers come in. They bring with them creativity, experience, and the ability to deliver a good set of plans.

A good architect or designer will take your ideas and offer options you might not have considered, working to develop a plan that works for you. She can also help you see on paper what the results of your remodeling will be. Making changes while they can be made with an eraser is far more desirable than asking someone to tear down what's been built because it isn't what you expected.

Your work together will result in a detailed set of plans that will be invaluable when the project is put out to bid. Plans that specify the type of air-conditioning unit, the finish on the cabinets, and the quality of wood for the deck will provide contractors with specifics upon which they can set an accurate price. And when you review the bids that come in, you'll be able comparing "apples with apples" because the contractors are all bidding on the same features.

If your construction is more than a small renovation, then the money you'll spend remodeling may be one of the major financial investments you'll make in your lifetime. Why do it without professional advice? With help, you'll have a space that fulfills your needs today while adding value to a future resale. In this chapter we'll outline which type of professional is right for your job, how to find ones to interview, and how to select the one who best suits your needs.

Design Professionals: Your Options

Practices vary throughout the country, but, in general, you'll find that you might turn to any of the following for help with your design work.

- **An architect.** Architects are licensed individuals who receive training in both artistic form and technical function so that your house is sound as well as attractive.
- **An independent home designer.** Some independent designers specialize in interior planning, so if you need help with the exterior as well be sure to verify that they have expertise in this area. They do not have the technical training of an architect, but if you've got a knowledgeable contractor this won't be a problem.
- **A designer employed by a kitchen or bath design firm.** These people work as part of a design-build firm and represent a specific product line. They have special expertise in designing these complex rooms.
- **A designer employed by a building supply store.** Some stores have staff designers who will help you plan your remodeling. The cost of the drawings may be included in a package price for the materials. If you decide to buy your materials elsewhere, there is usually a provision for buying the plans outright.
- **A design-build firm.** These firms offer one-stop shopping for home remodeling. They provide customers with design ideas and blueprints and will build the addition or renovation as well. Some companies are generalists who handle all types of remodeling; others specialize in kitchens or baths or both.
- **Your contractor.** In some parts of the country the use of a contractor for design work is the norm for all but the most extensive jobs.
- **Providing the plans yourself.** It's difficult for an untrained individual to turn out plans with all the necessary technical details, but you can do a lot of it yourself and then get some technical help by hiring a draftsman for the final blueprint, asking for help from your contractor or his staff, or using a first-rate computer program.

Who Should You Turn to?

Two elements will largely determine the type of design professional that's right for you.

The first is the size of the job. If you are doing a major home renovation anywhere in the country, then it is worth your time to seek out an area architect who does residential design. In addition to an artistic vision for your project, the right architect will have the education, training, engineering knowledge, and experience to guide you through the construction process and help you get the most for your construction dollar. Not only do they know what is going to go into the new construction, but they can figure out the best way to tie in to the old construction, working around poorly placed pipes, coping with old heating systems, and generally finding the best and most structurally sound way to accomplish the job without rebuilding the entire house.

Architects also know local building codes and zoning laws and can tell you that the extension you envision will require a zoning variance that may be hard to come by. Or they can tell you that, because you are building on a wet area, there will be added cost to putting in foundation for your addition—information that is handy to have from the outset.

The second factor in selecting the right type of professional is finding out what the practice is in your area. In and around major cities, architects specializing in residential work do large and small household renovations. In these communities, your referrals will probably be to architectural firms.

Elsewhere in the country, you may find that it is highly unusual for an architect to work on a residential project. In some states, signatures that would normally be provided by an architect can be provided by licensed engineers or even the contractor.

As you talk to people who have done work on their homes, you'll be able to determine who is filling the design function in your area. If you're planning to remodel a kitchen or bath, then people frequently turn to kitchen and bath designers. You may also get referrals to independent designers who are preparing plans for people. They may not have the in-depth technical training required of an architect, but they will offer experience, creativity, and knowledge that will help your project proceed smoothly.

Design-build firms are another possibility. These firms generally consist of designers and contractors who have teamed up to do projects. Listed in the Yellow Pages under "Remodelers" or "Home Improvement," these professionals can help you through the process.

Yet another source of design help is available in building supply companies, home-center "supermarkets," and some hardware stores. They frequently employ designers that advise customers on home projects. There is generally no fee for the initial store consultation, although there may be a $50 to $75 fee for an in-home visit.

Some building supply stores will provide drawings if you commit to purchase your supplies from them in return. If this is the case, try to do business with the store that offered the lowest price on materials, but ask them to guarantee their price quote through a certain date or ask that they cap any increase they may have to pass on to you. Get this agreement in writing.

In some areas, you will find that local contractors are providing design work for their customers. While a third-party designer offers the advantage of another perspective, a willing contractor has experience and can offer valuable advice. You'll find that they are prepared to work with you and to come up with a plan that is right for you. However, resist the urge to press your contractor into coming up with a design. If he isn't accustomed to doing it, you'll get a quick and easy addition (what a contractor is good at), but you may or may not be happy with the overall look.

HOMEOWNER TIP

No Planners Needed?

Most books on home renovation counsel that certain projects are small and don't require plans, and, because I represent the homeowner who wants and needs to save money, I would like to offer similar counseling—but can't do so wholeheartedly.

I sit on a local zoning board so I see several cases each year involving people who have hired carpenters to build decks or add small additions that they belatedly discovered required zoning variances. They have tried to put their home on the market only to discover that they can't because they have not obtained a variance. By law, a zoning board can request that the deck or addition be torn down before the home is put up for sale—certainly not a successful home improvement from the seller's viewpoint. A planner or architect would have helped them avoid this. Although I don't suggest that you hire an architect to design your deck, I tell this story to stress that for most homeowners this is new high-stakes territory in which an architect or planner often has unexpected knowledge that can be valuable in the long run.

I've also done bathroom renovations that consisted of nothing more than fixture replacement, but the overall bathroom was improved by a good plan. It was the architect who thought of a better placement for the heater. It was the architect who helped me solve some of the designs problems. And it was the architect who designed the vanity that is the focal point of the bathroom. If you've hired wisely, the money can be well spent.

CONTRACTOR TIP

Wanted: Good Plans

When I get a good set of plans from an architect or designer, it makes my job easier, and it can save the owner money. A well-conceived, well-drawn project can be built quickly and at less cost. Give me the brand name of the ceramic tile and the specifications on the water heater—just give me as much detail as you can. That way, I can build it for you better and faster. If you hire a contractor before these decisions have been finalized, it will cost you both time and money.

Selecting a Kitchen-Bath Design Firm

Like anything else, personal referral is the best method for finding good professionals. However, kitchen-bath firms have something else going for them, and that's product.

Most firms represent a certain line (or lines) of bath products or kitchen cabinetry, and if their showcase appeals to you you should be in safe hands getting your plans from them.

If you'd like to visit a few showrooms but you have no referrals, look in the Yellow Pages under "Kitchen Cabinets," "Kitchen Remodeling," or "Bath Remodeling." Some may display "NKBA" in their ads, certifying that they are members of the National Kitchen and Bath Association, a trade association that grants its emblem only to qualified designers. You can also get names by contacting the NKBA directly (see the resource section for more information).

NKBA designers have been trained for the work they do and must qualify to receive certain designations (certified kitchen designer or certified bath designer). The organization's code of ethics sets a high standard of professionalism, thereby reducing your risk when you do business with one of its members.

What's more, there's nothing like experience. If you were choosing between a designer who put together several hundred sets of plans for kitchens over the years and an architect who only designed kitchens sometimes, you might be well served by the person with the most experience.

The product's appeal and whether or not you like the designer who works with you will be the determining factors in success or failure of this design relationship. If you have any concern, ask about their policy regarding plans. Many of the firms prepare the plans at no extra charge; the cost is built in to the overall fee for remodeling. Some, however, will sell the plans if you decide to get the remodeling work done by someone else.

Most kitchen and bath design-build firms request 50% of the fee on signing, 40% at the time of cabinet installation, and 10% on completion. Some request a retainer at the time they start the plans, although the cost of the plans is later absorbed into the overall package.

Design-Build Firms

Design-build firms are often called "remodelers" or "remodeling specialists." If they are popular in your area, you'll probably be referred to one or find them listed in the Yellow Pages.

If you're hiring a design-build company, then your designer-salesperson will be your main contact for the job. You'll work together on the plan, and both designer and contractor will see you all the way through construction.

Check references, and refer to chapter 5 for additional suggestions on making your decision. Much of the advice concerning selecting a contractor will be applicable here.

The Design-Build Partnership

Any professional in the home remodeling business will tell you that the best remodeling projects come from a team approach, where the architect, builder, and homeowner get along well and become a single unit with an agreed-upon goal in mind.

Because it makes for a nice working relationship, some planners and contractors have teamed up for certain projects with homeowners they know, others have actually created full-service companies that offer the homeowner one-stop shopping for home remodeling.

Gone is the bidding process, which takes time and sets up an adversarial relationship from the beginning. In the bidding process, the contractor tries to interpret drawings to bring his price down to the lowest possible cost, then the owner tries to get the price down further. When this happens the independent contractor is left looking for gray areas where he can take shortcuts or reduce costs to get back the profit needed to make the job worthwhile.

If you have a friend who is a contractor or one who is a planner and you decide to create a design-build relationship for accomplishing your remodeling, one element above all others is necessary to make this relationship work: ethics. Because the homeowner is agreeing to work with a single architect and a single contractor, you need to have ultimate faith that you are working with people who are trustworthy. By linking the three of you, you are giving up your option of taking bids. If you trust the people with whom you're working, this is no problem. The three of you can work together to bring the job in at a good price. Just be aware that this is your team for going the distance. Be certain you're comfortable with them.

With this type of arrangement, the architect and contractor agree to a fixed fee, often 20% of the construction costs. There is no bidding and no project price. If the trio allows costs to get out of control, this will run up the homeowner's expenses. However, since the homeowner is in as an equal partner, there is no reason expenses should be run up unwittingly.

The following is an example of a family that decided to create their own design-build team. The homeowner did a small project with a contractor who he found to be well respected in the community, with the reputation of being above reproach when it came to ethical standards. When she decided to do another project, she asked the contractor to recommend an architect. The next item on the table was the dollar amount the family wanted to spend on the project. The architect went to work on rough drawings, comparing notes with the contractor, and before too long, the trio had agreed on an on-budget project that met the client's needs. The price was accurate because the contractor and architect worked together along the way, time was saved because the project didn't have to be put out to bid (or redrawn when it came in over budget), and harmony was achieved because the three agreed to work as a team.

Do-Some-of-It-Yourself Planning

If for some reason you are unable to locate an architect or planner that is right for you, or if you'd like to toy with what your idea might look like on paper, there are some tools you'll find handy.

Look for floor-plan kits at hardware stores and advertised in magazines to get started on a basic plan. You will still need help in planning your mechanical systems (plumbing, heating, electrical), and you'll still need a draftsman, a designer, or a contractor to help you with the details necessary to provide a working set of plans.

Investigate the adult education programs in your area. Many offer classes on home design and blueprint drawing. For the price of the course, you will gain valuable knowledge and experience, as well as the hands-on guidance of the instructor. If you have the time and the interest, it could be the best deal available for the price!

If you like computers, you'll actually have a great time working on some of the new programs that are available (see the resource section). These programs give you the ability to put together your own plans, and, if you work carefully, your paper results will compare favorably with a regular set of plans. The catch is that you still need your own personal sense of design and must be willing to do all the local research necessary to be certain that you've planned correctly.

If you want to tackle the plans yourself, it can be fun, but be certain that you give a professional (a draftsman or your contractor, for instance) the opportunity to examine them for any errors you may have made.

Finding the Right Independent Design Professional

Because design is a personal issue, seek out several names so that you'll have a variety of styles and personalities to choose from. For referrals, contact the following.

Friends and relatives. Talk to as many people as you can about your project. You know these people well, and if Aunt Edna, who is a detail freak, says that the planner thought of everything then you know that must be true.

Owners of homes you like. You may have driven past a home where they've done work you admire. (If the construction crew is still on site, one of them might tell you the name of the architect or design-er.) You might be able to find someone who knows the family, or knock on the door and ask the name of the architect. Few people object to questions that come with compliments.

Ideally, seek out referrals from people who have done work similar to what yours will be. The designer who developed a terrific plan for a 1991 home may not be the person to help you renovate a 1920s colo-nial; and if your home is a candidate for historic preservation, seek out an architect who has experience in this area. Keep in mind the scale of your project. If neighbors just had a luxury addition put onto their home and you're adding a basic bathroom for your kids, you may not want to interview their planner or architect. The struggle to keep your project appropriately priced may be too great.

The local chapter of the American Institute of Architects (AIA). Contact your local AIA office. Your state capital is a likely loca-tion for a chapter, but there may be other offices in your state. (If you have difficulty finding one, call the national office, listed in the resource section, to find the chapter nearest you.)

Some AIA chapters offer referrals to a short list of architects who fit the description you give them, others send out a state directory that lets you thumb through to find the ones nearest you. Directory listings also tell what percentage of the firm's work is residential.

"Architects are accustomed to traveling the state for jobs," says Suzanne Schwengel, vice president of the AIA chapter in Des Moines,

Iowa. "Though the headquarters may be in one city, there may be architects in practice in a community nearer to you."

Based on these referrals, select three of these architects or planners and set up appointments to meet with them. (If your list is more extensive, you might ask for literature and try to weed out firms based on the written material they send.) Many will meet with prospective clients for no fee, but be sure to ask.

Kitchen and bath designers frequently work out of showrooms, and your initial meeting may be there.

With independent planners, practices vary. Meetings held at the design professional's office have the advantage of letting you see her work, meetings at your home allow her to comment on the project you have in mind. Some will charge for this initial interview, so ask if there is a fee. They should be prepared to show you a portfolio of past work.

The Interview

The interview is crucial. You aren't buying a finished product that you can see, you are buying a service, and you are seeking someone who will provide guidance, good judgment, technical expertise, and creative skills at a reasonable cost. It's important to feel comfortable with this person.

At your meeting, be prepared to give a brief description of the kind of work you need done and give an idea of your budget. This is not the time to go into extensive detail on your project; it's your opportunity to assess whether or not this architect or planner has the time, desire, background, and creativity to solve the problems you describe.

Here are some of the questions you will want to cover:

1. What percentage of the design professional's (or the firm's) work is residential? Does the project described fall in line with the types of things the designer has done in the past?
2. What is their design philosophy? What sets them apart from the competition?
3. Describe a little more about your undertaking, and ask what this person sees as the important issues or considerations.
4. State the time by which you hope your project might be completed. Ask whether or not the planner might be able to fit you in on that schedule.
5. If you are interviewing someone from a firm, ask who you will be dealing with. Is this the same person who will be designing the project? If not, who does the design work?
6. How far do they generally take a project? Through the design phase? Into construction? Why?

7. What about overall costs? Do most of the projects come in on budget?
8. When it comes to fees, you'll want to know:
   - What is the fee structure?
   - If the scope of the project changes, how is the fee adjusted?
   - Is supervisory work during construction offered? Is it billed differently?
9. Can he estimate a fee for this project at this time? If not, when?
10. As a client, what will you see along the way? Will there be models, drawings, sketches? (Usually you can get any of these, but you will pay for the additional time to prepare what the firm does not consider standard.)
11. During construction it is very important to be able to reach the architect or planner immediately. Does she make special provisions for being reached by clients or contractors who have ongoing projects? How good is she about returning phone calls?
12. If you are interviewing architects, ask if they are members of the AIA. Membership means the architect subscribes to a professional code of ethics and has access to a variety of professional and technical resources.
13. If you need a person with a specialty in historic preservation or some other specific experience or qualification, be certain to discuss this.

What they ask you is also important. Does the designer or architect seem interested in you and your lifestyle?

At the conclusion of this meeting, you will want to ask for references and additional addresses of homes you might drive by to see more of the firm's work—preferably people who have done work similar to yours. References are particularly important for independent designers who are not architects, because there are no specific qualifications for setting up a business of this sort.

It's also a good time to evaluate the personal chemistry. Do you think you would enjoy working with this person? Did they seem to like and respect you? Were they on time? Did they seem well organized? All these factors are important in a working relationship.

If and when you set up another appointment to meet with a designer, reverse meeting locations. If you visited their offices on the first visit, then ask them to come to your home for the second. It's helpful to have met with them in both locations before making a final decision.

Checking Out Referrals

If you have a particularly positive feeling about one of the architects or planners, then his references should become your first priority. If you can, set up an appointment to see the space and to ask your questions. If you can't see the renovation and you have to ask your questions over the phone, then you'll still want to drive by the property. The renovation may be obvious from the outside, and, if not, at least you will have a reaction to the home. If it's well kept and generally makes a good presentation (even if it isn't exactly to your taste) seeing it will help you evaluate the homeowner's comments about the designer.

Be sure to call more than one reference. If they've given friends and relatives as their references, it will become apparent when you interview more than one person.

Most people who will be given as references will be disposed to tell you the good things. You'll want to listen for the bad, and there will be some. You can get at this a couple of ways: "If there was one thing about this project that you would have liked to have gone better, what was it?" Or: "Is there any advice you can give me about working with this designer?" (The fact that she is always late to appointments is the kind of information this question may elicit.)

Call references and say: "I'm thinking of using (blank) as a designer for some remodeling. Could you tell me:

- Did you enjoy working with him?
- Did you find the design ideas creative? Was he good at solving problems?
- How were initial price estimates? Did you feel that the firm knew what they were doing, or did you feel misled when it came to price?
- Did he meet deadlines? Was he good about following up on your concerns?
- Did your contractor seem to find it easy to work from the drawings?
- When you needed more information how was he about getting it to you?
- Was the job more or less on time?
- Did he get involved in construction?
- Was the planner or his staff easy to reach and responsive to phone calls during construction?"

How Costs Add Up

If you're interviewing independent planners or architects, you will pay for the time that the architect or planner must take to analyze your requirements, define what you need and want, develop and revise the design, coordinate the permit process, and ascertain that the project is built to specifications. You are also paying for someone to create a space that responds to you, to the site, and to the local climate.

In general, architects and some designers use one of four fee systems:

- hourly rate
- hourly rate with a cap—generally capped at some percentage of the construction cost.
- set fee
- percentage of the construction cost, generally 5% to 20%, depending on the services desired. (If you opt for a percentage, you must specify what the percentage is based on, for instance, just construction. If you're renovating a kitchen, will appliance costs be figured into the percentage, etc.?)

Often the fee is some combination of these. An architect or designer may work with both a flat fee and a percentage. Be wary of the percentage aspect, however. Remember that the more your project costs, the higher the fee that is paid to the architect. The only person who has an incentive to keep the price down is you.

Generally, architects use a fixed fee for the stage of the work over which they have most control, such as the design phase. Early client meetings or construction supervision are often billed at an hourly rate, because there is no way to control it. In general, architects want a down payment or retainer to establish the client's commitment to the project.

HOMEOWNER TIP

Listening between the Lines

When you speak to the references, really listen. I've been used as a reference by people I liked but I thought had professional weaknesses. I didn't want to trash the person, but I would have given fair warning to the potential client if they had been listening. Sometimes I've tried to give signals that there were problems, only to have my comment dismissed lightly by the caller. If you're only calling to have a good impression confirmed, then you haven't done your homework. Really listen to what the past client is saying, and if there is a word or a phrase that piques your curiosity pursue it. You may find that the person mis-spoke, or you may find that they were trying to tell you that as much as they loved Steve or Sue, there was a big problem when it came to permits or cost or whatever . . . Be certain you are receptive to what they are trying to tell you.

Expenses for which you may be billed include long-distance telephone calls and printing of blueprints and photography. These are often billed with a slight markup.

Always ask for an outline of the stages of work to be performed and the approximate cost of each.

Home renovation is an area in which costs can get seriously out of hand. Some are inevitable: your original house plans from the 1960s failed to show some pipes that now have to be relocated or the previous owner did the electrical work himself and it's not up to code. Those unexpected occurrences can and do happen. That said, you need to protect yourself from other unexpected costs by surrounding yourself with professionals who are cost conscious. If, during the initial interview, you sense a vagueness about money or if the references don't check out well when it comes to the financial end, run—don't walk—to another architect.

I can hear reader groans. . . . "Oh, but he's got such a great eye for design . . ." or, "But she did my neighbor's kitchen and it looks great." If

---

INSIDER'S TIP

Cost! Cost! Cost!

Once you've done your homework and are starting to have strong leanings toward one firm or person or another, there's one very important issue to consider: cost, cost, cost!

Architects and designers are notorious for being vague on costs. It is not unusual to hear stories of families whose projects come in from first estimate at triple to quadruple times the cost of what was originally discussed. Even when an amount is presented as a budget figure, costs can still get out of hand. The design professional has encouraged them to dream and to build up their wish list, and the client has unwittingly complied, innocently assuming that the architect is still working within the ballpark figure discussed initially.

Throughout this process, there are five words that you should say frequently—especially after each change discussed: "What's this going to cost?" This question should become second nature to you throughout this process. (You'll soon find that you'll have to ask it less often. Once the people you're working with become aware that you're watching closely, they'll begin to watch more closely too, and they'll be better at informing you as you go along.)

you have a bottomless purse, then working with this type of designer may be fine. However, be forewarned. It will be costly. One family wanted a new media-family room. When the plans came in, the contractors' estimates hovered around $320,000, four times what the couple had intended to pay! Another family dreamed along with their architect when renovating a kitchen and adding a portico. When they received

---

Designer/Architect Selection Form

Name_____Telephone_____

Firm name _____

Address _____

Heard about from (or referred by) _____

Specialties _____

Fee structure _____

Estimated cost/time_____

Client referrals

Name_____Telephone _____

Address _____

Comments_____

_____

Name_____Telephone _____

Address _____

Comments_____

_____

Other thoughts/follow-up questions _____

_____

Comments_____

_____

_____

_____

_____

prices, they not only had to pay to have the architect scale back the drawings, they eventually had to sacrifice the portico. They had become so wedded to some of the more expensive kitchen design elements, that they just couldn't give them up. As a result, they lost one of the major reasons they planned to do the renovation.

On a smaller scale, another family paid about double what the architect had estimated for a renovated bathroom. They breathed a sigh of relief when the architect specified a $120 wall sconce that would finish it off. At last, here was something that wasn't outrageously priced. However, when the light bulb burned out for the first time, the husband went to the store to buy a replacement and discovered that the fixture was foreign; the bulbs had to be imported and were quite expensive.

Don't Let This Be You

Architects point out that some clients exhibit the ostrich syndrome. They don't really want to know what things cost, or they want it to cost what they want to pay. "I had a client here the other day who was determined that he could have a double garage built for $10,000," says one architect. "I'd just done two similar projects and knew he'd never get it done for that price. Clients like this keep interviewing until they hear what they want to hear, but ultimately they have to pay the going price." When it comes to home contracting, there is no such thing as a free wall or free roof!

The Benefits of Being Cost Conscious

You may actually get a better result if you keep tabs on price. "It's easy to design something expensive," says an architect in Westchester, New York. "Designing something that's almost as good but costs less is a much greater challenge."

If you remind them that cost is an issue there will still be viable solutions, and the architect or planner will have to work a little harder to make it come out right.

Always remember, architects don't want to design something that doesn't get built.

Lining up Your Team

The best renovation projects grow out of teamwork. The architect or planner is an important team member who should share your enthusiasm and be happy to be on board.

Your next step should be to formalize your relationship with a contract. This will generally come from the architect, but, if not, the AIA has a standard contract that is a good, fair document on which to build.

Homeowner Checklist

Ask around for names of area architects and designers who are recommended by people you trust or who are responsible for homes you admire.

- Contact the local chapter of the American Institute of Architects for additional names.
- Make initial phone calls to firms to assess availability.
- Set up interviews with those firms that interest you. In addition to covering general questions, ask for a fee schedule for a project similar to the one you have in mind.
- After the interview, carefully check all referrals.
- Meet again with the architect whom you select. Verify that you are comfortable working together.
- Put it in writing.

Chapter 3

A Good Plan Can Make a Difference: The Design Phase

"Hammer" is to "nail" as "unexpected" is to "home renovation." When you open up a wall of a home, particularly an old one, it's almost inevitable that there will be elements you hadn't counted on—termite damage that somehow went unnoticed, pipes that are in need of replacement, not-to-code wiring that was obviously put in by some home handyman of long ago . . . the list of possibilites is endless. And if you're renovating an old home for which no blueprints survive, every-thing involved in the tying-in between the old house and the new remodeling will be filled with surprises.

That's why the design process is so important. Since you can't foresee the unforeseeable, it's important to anticipate and plan for everything that you can. You'll minimize the number of on-the-job surprises, and you'll maximize your chances of getting the results you want. What's more, you'll be in a better position to control costs by reducing the risk of encountering extra work that no one considered.

The Drakes are one family who wish they had understood the design process and worked through it more carefully. Their home, built in the 1940s, featured a small kitchen and a small dining room. To suit their modern family needs, they wanted to combine the two rooms and create a country-style eat-in kitchen that could become a family gathering place.

Wanting to maximize their construction dollar, they used a young freelance designer who was just starting out. "Her plans seemed good, and we loved some of her ideas for increasing our storage. It never occurred to us there would be a problem."

But the designer worked with standard measurements for the appli-ances, instead of specifically researching the pieces the family intended to use. When the refrigerator was delivered, it didn't fit in the intended location, so a new space had to be found. Ultimately, it was placed at the top of the basement stairs, not as conveniently located to the food preparation areas, and because the space is narrow the basement door must always be closed in order to open the refrigerator.

"We built some pantry storage to fill in the spot where the refrigerator was to have been placed, so that had its advantages," explains Deborah Drake, "but the location of the refrigerator is far from ideal. I really needed the larger model because of my teenagers, and by the time we discovered the problem, making room for the refrigerator would have meant changing several other elements. Ultimately, this was the best we could do, but I wish we hadn't encountered this surprise."

In this chapter, we'll outline the stages to expect during the design process, whether you're working with an architect, a designer, your contractor, or taking a shot at doing the drawings yourself. Throughout this process, you should be idea-gathering, and we've provided some suggestions on how best to research the elements you want in your home.

When you emerge from the design phase, regardless of whether you're hiring a pro or doing the plans yourself, you should have the following:

- detailed drawings of the work, preferably in blueprint form.
- a specifications sheet (sometimes a part of the plans) that provides detail—everything from the finish of the bookcases to the model and size of the refrigerator should be listed.

Communicating Your Dream

Refer again to your "Home Renovation" notebook where you've described what your goals are, as well as any extras you might like to accomplish—budget permitting. In all likelihood, you can now describe with some accuracy what your vision is and the elements you'd like your new space to contain. Expressing this clearly will be important in getting the design you want.

Consider any special requests you want to make during the design process. *The New York Times'* architecture critic, Paul Goldberger, explained in an article that he planned a major renovation for his summer home, and he sent the architect off with the stipulation: "Use stock items only." Though it was sometimes difficult to find the proper stock items, they eventually succeeded and all cabinetry and windows in the newly remodeled home were factory made. Custom work can greatly inflate the cost of anything, so it's certainly a sensible consideration.

Be prepared to describe how you live. Either you or a designer are custom-designing space *just for you*. In doing so, you ought to discuss questions such as the following:

- Who lives in this house?
- Do you have children? If so, what age are they?
- Do you have pets?

- When you are home, in what rooms do each of you spend the most time?
- How are the remodeled spaces to be used?
- Do you entertain frequently? Formally or informally?
- Do you have regular overnight guests, such as a mother-in-law who visits frequently?
- Is any furniture or appliance particularly important to you? It could be that your grandfather's "partner" desk is going to be a main feature in your home office. If you're designing a family room or media room of some type, your design should take into account any furniture that you intend to use, so that the room is large enough to accommodate those items.

There are also room-specific questions. If you're adding a home office, the designer ought to know of any special requirements of your business, as well as something simple like what you like to look at while you work. If you're remodeling a kitchen and you love to bake, the designer should take that into account when planning the space.

Special needs should be taken into account and accommodated whenever possible, without making it quirky or so individualistic that it would make it difficult to sell your home if and when the occasion arises. One couple tells of apartment-hunting in New York City and being taken to an apartment that was owned by a husband and wife, both of whom were over six feet in height. When the couple remodeled the kitchen, they made the counter height 4 inches higher than standard because it was more comfortable for them.

The prospective buyer, who stood only five feet, was amazed at being shown this apartment since the brand new kitchen would be very uncomfortable for a short person to use. When she quizzed the Realtor about having been shown this space, the Realtor replied: "I thought someone could build a little platform all along the counter base so that when you stood on it, the counter would be the right height." True story. Needless to say, no sale transpired that day.

For design considerations for specific rooms in the house, please refer to the next chapter.

If You're Working with a Designer or Architect

Once you've selected the designer or architect with whom you are to work, your next step is to convey your intentions. During this time, he should visit your home, discuss your lifestyle, and try to get a feel for exactly how you live so that the design can be both practical and visually pleasing.

Be specific about your goals. When the architect or designer asks for your wish list, say you want to talk money first. (If they design more than you want to pay for, you have to pay for the plans to be redrawn.) Give the designer an idea of some of the finishes you foresee using. (Formica or the more expensive Corian? Ceramic tile or linoleum? etc.) Then ask for a general budget figure. The architect can get a ballpark figure for you even with rough sketches. Once you know the general amount your basic plan will cost, you can better judge how many items on your wish list you might like to discuss.

Read the ideas in chapter 5: "While-Ya's and Honey-Do's." There may be some ideas there that you'd like to add.

As you talk, the architect or designer may have suggestions on better ways to accomplish your goals or to maximize the money you have to spend. Be open minded. So long as she has remained focused on your primary goals, you can benefit from her expertise.

The first thing you will see from a designer or architect will be the rough sketches.

Rough Sketches

This is the schematic design stage in which an architect may come up with two or three sketches of the project before going on with detailed drawings. (Some charge a set fee for a specified number of sketches.) He

---

HOMEOWNER TIP

Helping Your Architect Help You

A good architect can make all the difference in the quality and style of your remodeled home. However, you must keep your feet on the ground—and their feet, too—during the process. Keep checking with him or her on costs, and ask for an estimate based on the earliest drawings possible. Countless stories are told of plans that were submitted for bid and came in at double and triple what the homeowner's budget was. One family expected to spend about $120,000 on a new kitchen, family room, and exercise room. When the bids came in at $400,000 they were nothing short of flabbergasted. They were so angry and upset by having been led so far off course, that it was a full year before they had a new set of plans (by a new architect) ready to be put out for bid. Just keep asking, "How much?" They'll get the point.

may also consult with the local planning department or a structural engineer at this time to see if there are problems that would affect the design.

Ask the designer to walk you through the plans if there's anything you don't understand. At this stage, the drawings are generally simple, but that may be deceiving. Perhaps the designer has in mind a wonderful mantelpiece that will be the focal point of your new living room; that may come out in discussion rather than in the drawings.

This is your opportunity to get some new ideas on what you want to do. There will be things you like and dislike about the various sketches. For each, ask what the architect thinks are the pluses and minuses. In the time invested in drawing the sketches, he may have encountered some concerns. This is also a time to point out that you don't want to spend the money to move all the bathroom fixtures around; the renovation you had in mind would involve updating but leaving fixtures where they are to save on plumbing costs.

This is also the time to re-evaluate whether this is the designer for you. If you sense that the person hasn't a clue as to what you really want or if you get vague comments when it comes to price, you may want to rethink your relationship.

Communication is one of the most important elements in this entire process, and if you feel you're not communicating well this is a good time to look for another designer.

Design Development

Once a particular plan has been selected, the architect begins to prepare more detailed drawings. The floor plan will show all the rooms with the correct dimensions, and specifications for finish materials will be outlined. Heating and plumbing systems, materials, fixtures, and equipment will all be planned out.

Generally the architect reviews the proposed project with local agencies to allow for the orderly processing of applications. Permit drawings must be specific, and the designer needs to know of any problems that may crop up before going too far into the next stage.

It would be wise of you to verify with the architect or designer that this step has been taken. It does get overlooked occasionally, and it's a time waster if you have to do it belatedly. If you have any doubts, stop by the local building department with your drawings and double check.

As you review these drawings, consider how you will actually use the spaces. Ask yourself: Do the traffic patterns flow well? Does each space serve the intended purpose? Do I have a good sense of what it looks like? Will the furniture I have planned for each room work out? (Take measurements of your larger pieces of furniture and ask the designer to draw them to scale within the intended space.) Do I like how it looks?

Do I agree with the selection of wall and ceiling finishes, door types, windows, etc.?

This is when changes can be made with an eraser. Review every element with your designer or architect and be certain that you agree with the plan.

At this stage, an architect may also give drawings to a contractor for a preliminary cost estimate. If the costs are estimated to be much higher than anticipated, client and designer meet again to decide how to scale back. (This is why you don't want to attempt everything on your wish list; by the time you've come this far, cutting something out will feel like a major sacrifice!) Remember, too, you want this figure to be a little under the amount you really want to spend; the design specifications are not yet complete, and there are still the unexpecteds. If you've remodeled before, you know that it's awfully nice to have some money left at the end to spend on decorating.

Construction Documents

Now come the fully detailed drawings, the plans that will provide your contractor with the how-to instructions he needs to realize your vision. Everything from depth of excavation to type of nails and the finish on any built-ins should be specified at this time; the more details the better. One woman tells of arriving home from work to find that all the light switches in her home had been placed "where ever"—where ever it was convenient for the workers. "I learned the hard way how important it is to spell everything out," she notes.

To help your designer come up with plans that are detailed, discuss specifics. Ask about the heating system that is specified; remind him or her that you have a family with a lot of electrical gear (computers, audio equipment, etc.) and you'll need adequate wiring; ask about the hot water heater, what model and size he or she is specifying and why. If you've researched the specific air-conditioning unit you want, make sure it's noted. You don't want the contractors who bid on the job to allow for the unit they normally use; you want it priced for the unit you plan to use. Only by making certain that all of these elements comply with what you want can you be sure that the contractor will have a set of plans that accurately reflects what you have in mind.

Once you have these documents, read them carefully. (See the section on reading blueprints in the Appendices.) This is the instruction book for remodeling your home, and you want to be certain that you understand and agree with everything. No detail is too small to question. Particularly for technical details, ask about repairs: If something goes wrong with the air-conditioning unit (or heating, etc.), is it constructed in such a way that it will be easy to repair?

These documents will eventually become part of the construction contract and be submitted for the building permit at this time.

HOMEOWNER TIP

Listening to the Pro

We learned about Brenner Builders because Kevin was doing a small job for one of our next door neighbors. He heard about our intentions and followed up regularly to find out if we had plans ready yet. When our plans were ready, we submitted them to four contractors recommended by our architect and one to Kevin.

Although we had "discovered" him, the fact that we hired Brenner Builders was largely due to the rec-

ommendation of our architect, who had never before met him. When the bids came in, two were very close. Our architect knew the other contractor and was getting to know Kevin, and ultimately he recommended that we give this new fellow a try.

Brenner Builders was at that time unknown in this community, and knowing that he'd won over our architect certainly made us feel more secure in giving him the job.

Hiring a Contractor
While the selection of the contractor is ultimately made by the homeowner, the architect can offer recommendations as to who should be included in the bidding process. If you've hired your architect or designer to see you through this phase, then he will send out the plans and phone contractors to remind them of the deadline for submitting bids.

The selection of the contractor will be fully discussed in a following chapter, but suffice it to say that an architect can help you weigh the pros and cons in making your decision.

Supervising Construction
Once construction begins, there will be times when the homeowner is relieved not to have to navigate all the decisions alone.

"You can't draw everything, nor can you foresee all that can happen during construction," says one architect. "There will always be field decisions to be made, and the involvement of an architect insures the integrity of the project." This is often viewed as an optional aspect of an architect's service, and for this reason fees are sometimes on an hourly basis.

If you use an architect for construction administration, she is not on site all the time, although she will do regular site inspections. The architect is also available for consultation on issues that arise: What do you do when the crew discovers a steel beam in a wall that was to come down? How should the workers make up for a two-inch slope over the 25-foot expanse where an old hardwood floor meets a new hardwood floor? The skylight has to be placed a little differently because of attic wiring, so how should it be situated? These are items that an architect can help with as the job proceeds.

If You're Working on Plans with Your Contractor

If contractors in your area customarily provide plans for remodeling, then that is a perfectly acceptable route to follow. (If you're doing historic preservation or an extraordinarily complex remodeling job, then you still might be wise to contact the American Institute of Architects in your state for additional help.)

Contractors bring to the planning stage a great sense of practicality. You'll gain advice from someone who builds things regularly, someone who can tell you what makes sense and what doesn't. (There are times when that's far preferable to listening to someone tell you how a cathedral ceiling will improve your baby's bedroom.) You'll also save some money. What you lose is a third party coming up with some solutions for the space problem or design dilemma. You can compensate for this loss to some degree by taking it slowly and trying to think through each stage in advance.

Basically, the stages are somewhat the same, but the process will be slightly different.

Rough Sketches
Most contractors prefer that you come up with the first rough sketch of the design. They want to build whatever you like, but you will need to have a good idea of what that is. (See below for additional information on drawing up your design.)

Design Development
This is where the contractor takes over and shows you what is practical. Some contractors have draftsmen who will work with you on your plans. Others use computer programs, so what she may come back to you with will be a computer generated design showing what you've drawn in rough sketch.

Regardless of the type of drawing, this will be the time when the contractor may show you that the entry to a new room would be better in a different place, or that because of the way the plumbing runs in your house, it is cheaper to locate the new sink in a place different from what you planned. Open discussion and adjustments should be made at this time.

Construction Documents
The builder will need to generate specific plans to submit to your local building department. Laws vary by locale, but generally before plans are

submitted an architect or an engineer must sign off on the structural soundness of the plans and verify that they comply with local zoning ordinances. Most contractors who provide plans have a system for this; there is usually a separate fee for the person who reviews the plans and provides approval, so ask what it is.

The more detailed the building plans, the better it is for you. This is your opportunity to check that what you have in mind and what the contractor has in mind match. As when working with a designer, it's also your opportunity to evaluate the placement of everything from windows to electrical outlets. Changing things now is much easier than changing them as they are being built.

Good plans will also help you as you go through construction. Although there won't be a designer or architect looking over the builder's shoulder, you will be certain that he's building according to plan because you'll have the drawings in hand.

If You're Designing the Plan Yourself

Some people know exactly what they want and want to take the drawings as far as they can until they need technical advice regarding some of the mechanical elements of home design.

If you'd like to give the job a try, here are some things to keep in mind.

If you're designing on a computer: If you have a computer and enjoy using it, you'll probably have a good time working with one of the "home architect" programs. You may want to start out with one of the basic plans provided and adapt it to your needs, or you may want to start out with a "clean screen" and design the environment yourself. The programs have become quite sophisticated, and once you've devised your basic plan there are ways that you can even add details such as the electrical work. By dragging and clicking, you can create an accurate plan, and the best part is that you can change any aspect of it the next day!

Some of the programs even have the design equivalent of "spell check." Aptly titled "Plan Check," the program scouts through your plan looking for errors that you ought to correct. You may soon discover that you missed your calling and that you were actually destined to be the next Frank Lloyd Wright. (See the resource section for more information on computer programs.)

If you're drawing by hand: Use graph paper and develop a scale for drawing. Normal blueprints are done on a scale of $1/4$ inch to one foot. Select a scale that will work for the size of your project and be consistent.

- Begin your design by drawing the exterior perimeter wall to scale. Many amateur designers forget that exterior walls have

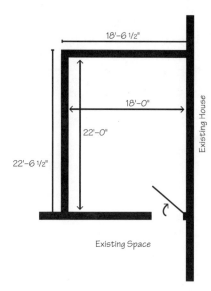

18'-6 1/2"

18'-0"

22'-0"

22'-6 1/2"

Existing House

Existing Space

depth. If you are planning an addition, allow approximately $6^1/_2$" for wall depth. Therefore, a new room with exterior dimensions of 10' × 12' becomes a room 9'1" × 11'1" of workable interior space. As you draw the windows and doors exactly where they are, note how doors open. This will prevent one door from colliding with another.

- Don't forget to add closets. Even if you are planning to use the room as a home office, a closet will be handy as well as important when it comes to resale.
- Measure your furniture and see if it's going to fit as you intend it to.
- Contact your local building department. They may have someone who can help you with planning the electrical, plumbing, and heating systems so that they are to code. They may also refer you to an engineer who specializes in helping people with this, for a fee. Although there will be code requirements for these mechanical elements, sketching in where you anticipate having appliances or lights or televisions will allow you to figure out where you need wall switches, overhead lights, and telephone jacks.

Rather than sketching from scratch, you might want to try one of the planning kits mentioned earlier. They come with a grid board, manual, and reusable peel-and-stick symbols for everything that you need.

Before getting started, you might consider whether or not there's an adult education course in your area on home design or blueprint drawing. These courses can provide you with a wealth of information, and the course instructor can function as consultant on what you are planning.

Completing Your Plans

After you finish your plans, put them away for a few days. When you get them out again, you'll have more to add and you'll see elements that you might not have noticed otherwise.

Next, show them to friends whose taste you admire and walk them through what you have in mind. Chances are you'll get some good suggestions.

Your contractor may be willing to turn your plans into construction documents, or your computer document may be good enough to take directly to an engineer or architect for approval. Drafting companies will also provide finished blueprints. Ask your contractor or the building department. For a few hundred dollars, they will put all necessary structural information into the plans including detailed cross-sections and diagrams of the electrical, plumbing, and heating elements. If you are doing major work or complex work like altering existing foundations, digging out or expanding a basement, or raising the roof, the fees are worth it.

You'll also need to prepare a specifications sheet that provides info on bath fixtures, paint color, etc.

Getting Local Approval

Regardless of who does your plans, you will need a building permit that requires a set of plans that are specific enough that the building inspector can come to the site and see that what you've built is what your plans said you were building.

You may also have to use your plans to gain approval from other local boards. If your addition is too close to your property line or in some way violates local code, you will need to appear before the zoning board of appeals. In addition, many communities have architectural review boards or neighborhood associations that require that you gain their approval on changes as minor as replacing a regular window with a bay window. While this may seem irritating, remember that you have selected this community and one of the advantages is that the regulations guarantee that your neighbors will never be able to build the Taj Mahal on their property.

If you're working with a local architect, you should be getting excellent advice about the process. Good local architects have a pretty good idea of what the local boards like and dislike and can tell you when and how to go about getting approval. Architects generally like to go in with a preliminary set of plans that are very specific as to measurements and building details but may not yet be fully completed in terms of additional specifications. That way if modifications must be made, at least they are made before everything is "set in stone." While the local zoning board doesn't need to know your floor finish or your sink choice, they do need to know exactly how large that skylight you're installing is, or exactly how far the bump out for your kitchen is going to be. If the drawings are not satisfactory, they can postpone their decision and wait for you to submit more detailed drawings. If you have any concerns, check them out with someone in the building department.

You must successfully navigate this stage, or you will be unable to do the work you intend. For that reason, it's worth taking seriously. Talk to people who have appeared before the board and speak to the local building department. If your request is emotionally charged (neighbors

don't want you to add a garage so close to their property), you may
need to hire a lawyer. (Hire someone local who knows the board and
has successfully helped people in the past.)

In some communities you may present your case alone, or, depending on the case, you may want your architect or designer and attorney
to present it. By all means, be clear, be polite, and provide documentation. A set of plans and photographs of your property and neighboring
properties (if appropriate) will be helpful. They may ask some prickly
questions, and those should be answered clearly and politely. (It will do
you no good to respond in irritation or anger, even if they are out of
line with a question. Your hot headedness could cost you the variance
or the approval you need.)

If yours is a difficult case and your neighbors are concerned, a good
board may even serve as mediator for the neighborhood. They know
you will be angry if you are denied a reasonable variance, but they don't
want your neighbors to be angry either. Ultimately, everyone has to live
together so it's important that you—and your neighbors—help get the
matter straightened out.

With architectural review boards and neighborhood associations, you
have more room to negotiate. These people are community volunteers
who may enjoy making suggestions that would optimize your project
despite the fact that it might cost $50,000 more. State your case. If you
considered their suggestion and rejected it, explain why. If it isn't practical, explain that, too. Always be polite. They do have the power to make
you come back after redesigning something, so do all you can to be
firmly pleasant on what you won't be able to do.

There will be a fee for the building permit, and requests for variances
cost as well. Fees vary throughout the United States; in San Francisco a
building permit for a deck in 1993 cost $244, and if a variance was nec-
essary it was a total of $705. In contrast, that same deck could have
been built in Atlanta, and the building permit would have cost $30, and
if a variance was necessary the cost would have gone up to $100. Call to
find out what your local costs will be.

Doing Research and Building Knowledge

"Gee, I didn't think of that" are bad words to have to utter right after
you've finished remodeling. This is a major undertaking, and you ought to
end up with what you want so take the time to explore all your options.

- Visit model homes in your community. Seeing a few model
  homes will show you what customers presently value in new
  construction. Maybe you'll value it, too. Or if the salesperson
  says, "work islands in the kitchen are really big right now," it

may make you re-evaluate the use of your space. You'll get an idea of what's happening now and what you might easily do to update your home.

- Keep reading those home design magazines. Every time you go through the grocery store checkout line, skim through the new issue of the latest remodeling magazine. It may give you some new ideas.
- Keep talking to friends and visit their homes if you can. By visiting, you get to see firsthand what works and what doesn't. You'll also find that people remember more details to share with you when you're right there in the space they've created. Suddenly they'll tell you that the skylight that looks so terrific leaked for the first year that it was in and that it took several visits to get the problem corrected. All these factors will help you make a judgment as to whether or not it's something you want to do.
- Visit showrooms and ask lots of questions. If you buy this brand of tub, is there a matching sink and toilet? (Sometimes there isn't!) Ask what happens if something breaks or must be replaced. How readily can it be fixed, and on replacement, is there a delay while the item is sent from Europe? You need to know the downside of everything. Getting total costs is important, too. Often there are hidden costs that the layperson could never anticipate, and you ought to know about those before selecting a brand.

  A final question for the showroom or store representative should be: "I really don't know much about buying (blank). Is there anything else I should think about or consider?"
- And of course, a good follow-up question is always: "If you were choosing between these two or three items, what would you put in your home?" Here's where you may find out about excellence in service, easy-to-clean features—the qualities you value when you're actually using the item.
- Keep adding this information to your "Home Renovation" notebook. If you're remodeling more than one room, set up dividers so that you have a section for each room. Keep brochures, notations regarding appliances, wallpaper samples, paint swatches, and other finishing design elements for each room in separate pocket dividers.

Overall, the most successful home remodeling projects are ones that take the vocabulary of the old house and use it creatively. Your ranch house could never become a Tudor, and a cupola is going to look out of place on anything but a Victorian. As you go through the process of remodeling, consider what attracted you to buying your current home. Those are the elements that should be enhanced with your new design.

A well-designed renovation is one in which the new is added so seamlessly that you can hardly tell it from the old.

One Good Thing We Did

We almost did enough toilet research. We had the misfortune to get our building permit the week that the new state law regarding low-water flush toilets went into effect. It's a complicated story, but we ultimately decided we'd better consider power-flush toilets for our new bathrooms. However, we'd heard they were very loud. "How loud?" we'd ask. "Well, loud," said the showroom representatives.

"Can we flush one?" we asked at a showroom. Showroom toilets are for display, not for testing, but they were nice enough to tell us of a supply house where they had one we could test.

HOMEOWNER TIP

How Not to Do Research

While my excuse is three kids, a dog, and a work life are the reason I wasn't always on top of my research, of course, the only one I can hold responsible for this negligence was me—and was I negligent on some recent shopping for remodeling! Here are some of the areas where I went wrong. Learn from my mistakes!

Mistake # 1: Actually this was less a mistake than a case of what I think is artful deception on the part of the showroom I visited. For two bathrooms I was remodeling, I selected some lovely hardware. The faucets and showerheads were wonderful, and I could afford the marked price. What I never suspected (and no one told me) was that with some European hardware, you pay in addition for all sorts of accessory parts that are necessary for the hardware to function properly. I left the showroom, satisfied with my decision and thinking that the marked price was my price (and that my plumber would get a discount). Well, my plumber went to the supply house, picked up what I ordered to the tune of quite a bit more than I had anticipated. The bill now included the faucets I picked, plus 99 little items that were needed to make it actually work. What's more, because it was an unusual make, the first time out the plumber put it together upside down and it took a lot of time to get it worked out. Ask all you can about the items you purchase.

Mistake #2: I didn't ask about items that matched. I was lucky that my tubs and sinks matched,

We arrived at the plumbing supply house on Christmas Eve. The company had a full spread of food for their plumber customers in honor of the holiday, and into this cheerful atmosphere we walked, asking to try their power-flush toilets. The fellow to whom we spoke gave us a look and then told us to wait a minute. He conferred with a fellow worker, then they both strolled back to where we waited, saying: "Fine. The only thing is it's in the men's room." I blushed and shoved my husband in the direction they were pointing, and then they got involved and decided that I should go back, too. Well, after that, what were we going to do?

George and I walked back, flushed the toilet a few times, looked as satisfied as we could, thanking them as we slunk out. Embarrassing it was, but we had our answer! Loud was loud, but not too loud.

HOMEOWNER TIP

How Not to Do Research (continued)

despite being manufactured by different makers. I had less luck with my accessories. Because the line was new in the United States, they had created a tub faucet but no over-drain pieces for U.S. tubs. I had to settle for a close match on brass in order to finish off the tub. (If I'd known to ask the question, the answer might have given me the red flag to select another brand, a move that would have saved me a bundle.)

Mistake #3: We didn't shop around early enough. Some wonderful work is being done in appliances and features, such as vanities. Had I gone to my architect or contractor with the specific sink, vanity, or some major ready-made piece I wanted to use, he could have more easily designed around a major item I liked and could afford.

As it was, we created a space, and then had to use custom-made items because nothing else fit.

Mistake #4: We forgot to ask, "What do we do when this new-fangled thing breaks down?" (I won't continue this saga any longer, but the highlight was six weeks with no toilet and about $400 in plumbing bills to have the under-warranty toilet replaced.) I'll cut to the chase: Would I put this toilet in my house again? Yes. It is a good product and the repair problems will improve as they appear in more and more houses. The moral here is to become an "Eternal Student of Remodeling." Keep visiting, shopping, and listening so that you can acquire the knowledge you need to manage costs while still coming up with the remodeling results you want.

Homeowner Checklist

- Be specific with your designer or architect as to what you want and what you can pay.
- Work closely with her during design development.
- Read the plans carefully at each stage; be sure you understand them.
- Read and understand the plans for the mechanical installations, too.
- Seek local approval if necessary.
- Continue researching elements you'd like in your remodeled space.
- After the design phase you should have: detailed drawings, usually blueprints, and a specifications sheet detailing all finishes and materials for your project.

Chapter 4

"I Wish I'd Thought of That!"

"The biggest mistake we made was not having them excavate a full base-ment. Now we've got three kids, and we really could have used the space."

"We were pennywise but pound-foolish about quality," says another homeowner. "We chose some less expensive materials to save money, which would have been fine if we'd really verified quality. As it was, some of the things, like the kitchen floor, really began to show wear sooner than they should have."

"We chose a temporary solution to the problem of water in our base-ment by having the contractor install a sump pump," says a regretful homeowner. "We should have spent the extra money to have them dig around the foundation and excavate a footing drainage system while we had the equipment there and the yard was a mess. As it was, we had to bring them back to do the work later, and it was a mess—again."

To go through months of remodeling only to realize that you wish you'd done it differently is a terrible feeling. This chapter is a compendi-um of remodeling suggestions and design ideas that might help you avoid those nagging feelings of regret. For easy reference, check off those ideas that seem particularly useful to you.

General Construction Suggestions

☐ If you're doing new construction for an addition, price out the cost of adding a full basement. Barring the discovery of rock or swamp, in most homes you can get a full basement (finish it off later) for a small increase in cost.

☐ If you're putting on an addition and you own a two-story home, add two stories, not just one. Roughly the same footing and foun-dation are required, and you'll gain almost double the square footage for not that much more money. An increase in square footage also elevates the value of your property.

☐ Put money into structural elements now so that you won't have to do it later. Your first remodeling dollars should go toward making your home sound and weathertight. If the roof is old, a beam is rotting, or the electrical system needs to be updated, budget for those corrections. If you do the cosmetics first, chances are you'll be ripping out new bathroom tile in a couple of years in order to repair a burst pipe.

☐ Your plans can be creative and interesting but search for alternatives that can save you money by simplifying the design. If the architect suggests a round deck (it's hard to build "round"), ask about building a hexagonal deck instead—an interesting design at a far lower cost.

☐ Invest in the best materials you can afford. You won't see the workers after the job is done, but you will see the cabinetry or tile.

☐ While today's drywall has its advantages when it comes to construction, it's lacking when it comes to creating sound barriers between rooms. You can improve this by requesting a slightly heavier grade of drywall or paying what is a minimal amount in the long run for the installation of insulation in your walls. The added insulation cuts down on the noises of telephone conversations, stereos, televisions, etc.

☐ You can take this a step further by installing exterior-grade doors between rooms where you really want to break sound. Sound buffers can also be created with bookcases or by placing closets or staircases between rooms.

☐ When insulating, spend the extra few dollars for R-30 insulation (instead of R-19). You'll see a noticeable difference in heat loss and sound-reducing elements.

☐ Examine your technical plans as carefully as you do the blueprints for your floor plan. These elements can be equally crucial to the success of your project.

☐ If you're extending your heating system or adding a new one and will have a new thermostat, consider carefully where you put it. One homeowner made the mistake of locating an upstairs thermostat at the head of the stairs. It catches all the heat that rises from downstairs and shuts itself off before the bedrooms have received adequate heat.

☐ Alarm keypad placement is also cause for thoughtful consideration. Although the master bedroom appears to be a prime location for an upstairs control, a smart alarm installer will look around for children, pointing out: "When she's 17, do you really want her coming in here at midnight to set the alarm for the night?" Perhaps there's a hall location that is easily accessible to all members of the family.

☐ Heating and plumbing pipes in exterior walls require careful insulation to prevent freezing. Be sure that the contractor has provided for this.

☐ Save money by using stock items whenever possible. There are some wonderful things around if you look.

☐ If replacing windows, investigate the style that tilts in for easy washing.

☐ If you're building a screened porch on an open deck, have screening material installed under the floor of the deck. Otherwise, all the bugs you deflect from above will simply take an underground route to get in.

☐ Windows with paned glass are so expensive that they're becoming a thing of the past. To achieve the divided-light look people are using snap-in grilles over full-expanse windows, which are easier to clean and less expensive.

☐ Plan for lots of storage. Everyone always wants more.

Overall Floor Plan

A good floor plan usually divides the home into three basic areas:

1. Working or high-activity zones, such as the kitchen
2. Moderate-activity zones like the family room
3. Sleeping zones

The working areas should be grouped together away from sleeping zones. As you consider household traffic patterns, observe how you get from area to area. A poor design is one in which you have to walk through bedroom halls to go from the family room to the kitchen.

☐ If you do not currently have a bathroom on the main floor, this may be the time to consider putting one in. Not only will it be convenient for you now, but you'll be glad you did it when you're ready to sell.

☐ A main entry to a home should be light, airy, and welcoming. A secondary entry should be functional: Consider hooks for the kids coats and backpacks, space for boots and frequently used sporting equipment, and an area where you can temporarily place items such as dry cleaning or packages to be taken to the post office.

☐ Many people today prefer to have the laundry room upstairs nearer the bedrooms. Laundry facilities in the kitchen were popular for a time, but, with this plan, consider that you may have to finish folding the clothes before the kids can sit down for a snack.

Room Floor Plans

Here are some important questions to consider.

TRAFFIC PATTERNS

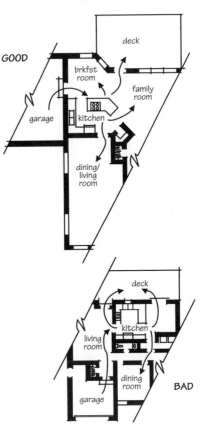

☐ Who is going to use the room?

☐ Will the windows you envision provide adequate light and good ventilation?

☐ Based on where you see the placement of doors, how will the traffic pattern flow? Does it make sense? (See floor plans at right for examples of good and bad traffic patterns.)

☐ What furniture do you envision in the room? What size is it? Some walls that currently appear blank may be broken up by air ducts and radiators, so be certain these elements have been placed before you consider furniture layout. If it's a family room, decide where the couch and the TV will go; if it's a bedroom, consider placement of bureau and bed. (Bedrooms should have at least two walls that are uninterrupted by doors or low windows.)

☐ What kind of storage needs will the room require? Even rooms that don't normally require storage could use some. If you'll have bookcases in the living room, consider closing in some lower shelves for other types of storage. A dining room might benefit from built-in storage for dishes. A family room should have a good-sized closet for games and supplies used in that room.

General Design

☐ One often overlooked but extremely important aspect of any home is the lighting, and it's often an afterthought. As you plan, take into account what time of day various parts of your home get sunlight. Consider what windows you may lose as a result of the addition, and consider all other window placement. Skylights may be an option to brighten a room but leaks can and do occur, and in warm climates they may simply raise the indoor temperature.

☐ Once you've explored natural lighting, ask lots of questions about other ways to light a room. Torchieres, some using halogen bulbs that give off an intense but natural bright light, have opened up new options for increasing room lights.

☐ Particularly in rooms like kitchens and baths, envision the final product. The selections made during construction regarding flooring and tile will greatly influence the overall decoration of the room. Will you be able to find accessories that go with your color scheme? And while you certainly shouldn't design your renovation for the sake of resale, keep in mind that the strange and unusual may prevent your home from selling. If lime-green appliances in the kitchen were your first choice, you may want to reconsider. Flexible, functional colors generally sell better.

Kitchen

Putting money into remodeling your kitchen is a good investment. According to *Remodeling* magazine, kitchens are the number one remodeling project when it comes to return on investment. Keep in mind, too, that kitchens are extremely complex. One designer of upscale kitchens notes that it can take six months to plan a kitchen that will only take four months to build. Do your homework so that you'll benefit in the long run. Keep the following in mind as you plan.

☐ If you'll be reconfiguring how the kitchen will match up with the rest of the house, keep in mind that you want easy access to the kitchen from a back door or the garage (for bringing groceries in, for example) and easy access to the dining room, breakfast area, family room, and deck.

☐ Some houses are designed so that you have to walk through the kitchen to get to a basement recreation room or to get to the family room or to go out the back door. If the traffic pattern through your kitchen is heavily used, this should be considered as you select your work space and place your appliances. Try to avoid a layout that means the family has to traipse back and forth through your work path.

☐ Within the kitchen, you'll need at least three areas:

Food preparation area. You'll want counter space with space to store utensils, food processor/mixer, cutting board, measuring devices, and storage for plates and bowls nearby.

Cooking area. This should consist of counter space near the range and oven.

Clean up area. The center of this area will be the sink and garbage disposal with the dishwasher and trash receptacle nearby.

☐ Most kitchens are designed in a triangular formation: sink, refrigerator and stove all within convenient reach of each other. Typically, the traffic pattern in a kitchen is from the refrigerator to the sink and the range to the sink. For that reason, it's best to put the sink between these two points. The following are some points to consider when planning the kitchen:

☐ How many cooks must you allow space for?

☐ Do you need an eat-in kitchen?

☐ How many ovens do you need?

☐ Can you save money by giving your cabinetry a cosmetic face lift instead of replacing it?

☐ Many people like a window over the kitchen sink. Will this work with your layout?

☐ If you have a kitchen island, be sure that your dishwasher has clearance and won't hit it when open.

☐ Can you get into your oven and microwave conveniently, even when others are in the kitchen?

☐ Can you provide for dish storage near the dishwasher to make putting away easier?

☐ Can you get from stove to sink without obstruction?

☐ Are outlets well located for where you want your toaster, mixer, etc.?

☐ Do you plan to store any appliances on the kitchen counter, or would you like under-counter storage for as many items as possible? If you need counter storage for a something like a heavy mixer, consider the appliance garages they are creating now. (This type of storage area features a pull-down door from the overhead cabinet to the countertop and encloses an appliance.)

- [ ] Some people want a desk, space for homework, ironing, and a room where their guests can follow them when they are entertaining. Do you want a kitchen that provides for any of these needs?

Here are some other tips and suggestions:

- [ ] Make sure sink access won't be blocked when the dishwasher is open.
- [ ] Refrigerator doors should always hinge away from the sink and stove or cooking surface.
- [ ] Create space behind a closed door for recyclables.
- [ ] Create as much storage and counter space as possible. You'll want counter space on both sides of the sink and the range and on at least one side of the refrigerator.
- [ ] Visit kitchen showrooms to get ideas on all the different types of storage systems available. From pull-out shelves and built-in wine racks to a flip-down, under-sink board where you can stash sponges, soap, and dish-scrubbing materials, there are many new things available. Pick and choose what will work for you.
- [ ] An island in the center of the kitchen offers the social advantage of bringing people to the center of the room instead of everyone working with their back to each other.
- [ ] Purchase easy-to-clean materials for the kitchen.
- [ ] Try to see flooring that's in use. For a time, a rubber flooring with raised bubbles was popular, but anyone who saw it in use (it was also installed in many stores) realized that while the bubbles were relatively easy to clean, the dirt that slipped down between was almost impossible to remove easily. To give this flooring a good cleaning you really needed to get down on your hands and knees and use a scrub brush! Even if the flooring or tile or other material that you're considering is gorgeous, look at it from a practical standpoint. Will it show spills? Will it wear well? Will I be able to clean it?
- [ ] If you use a cooktop, locate a drawer for utensils under it.
- [ ] Consider lighting. Some people like under-counter lighting. It's a nice touch, but it isn't vital unless you have a particularly dark area or discover that you'll cast a shadow over your work surface.
- [ ] Today's families like building kitchens off "Great Rooms" (a space with room for the family to sit comfortably and watch television). Often at the rear of the home, Great Rooms frequently feature a wall of windows. When the remodeling is completed, the family discovers that there is no logical space

for the television and absolutely nowhere for a wall unit to hold other media items. Prethink the use of your room when you plan your space.

☐ When considering a Great Room, consider, too, the age of your children. If you have a baby or toddlers, it may sound like a good idea to create a space where they can play safely while you fix dinner. However, there may come a time when you all like your 6 P.M. space. If there is an alternate room they can use for watching television or talking on the phone, you might actually get to watch the news while fixing dinner. Despite how you feel now, there will come a time when you might find it pleasant to separate for 30 minutes before a meal.

☐ Walk through several kitchen activities while studying the floor plan to see if it works for the things you do. How will you remove the vegetables from the refrigerator? Does the refrigerator open the most convenient direction? Take the vegetables to the sink to wash them (where will you keep the colander?), and then do the cutting (is the cutting area near the sink for easy disposal?). When you bring dirty dishes to the sink where will you put them until it's time to load the dishwasher? Is there still a logical spot to organize dessert and coffee, if you have not yet done the dishes?

☐ Ask the contractor to save your old kitchen cabinets and install them elsewhere in the house: They can provide you with storage and a folding surface in the laundry room; or storage and workspace in the basement or garage.

The Bathroom

The square footage for most bathrooms is small, so consider this an exercise in space management.

If you're remodeling rather than building new, it is always cheaper to leave the sink, toilet, and tub where they are. Once you start moving fixtures, the dollars mount. That said, if there's something about the current placement that really bothers you, now is the time to ask what the job would cost and consider whether it's worth the higher price.

Consider what you want in a remodeled bathroom:

☐ Do you want a shower only, a tub only, a shower-tub combination, or both separately?
☐ Do you have adequate storage space? Adequate countertop space?
☐ Is there a place for towels and toiletries?
☐ Would you like more than one sink, and do you have space for it?

☐ Create under-sink or closet storage for bathroom cleaning products (spray, sponge, toilet brush). It can make cleanup much easier.

☐ A built-in laundry hamper or a place to tuck one in a closet gets one more item out of the way.

☐ Create a spot to tuck a wastebasket behind closed doors.

☐ If space is not an issue, double the usability of a bathroom by adding privacy walls or doors between fixtures. Two people can use the same space in relative comfort.

☐ Bathrooms seem larger with a window. Consider using glass blocks, which provide light and privacy. Skylights are also nice.

☐ If there is no window, a fan for ventilation is generally required by code. It will extend the life of your bathroom because humidity build-up from the shower is destructive to walls and paint.

☐ For additional privacy, have the room fully insulated, even if it's an interior room. The insulation will provide a sound buffer that you'll appreciate for years to come.

☐ A grab bar in shower and bath increases safety.

☐ If your walls will be painted or papered, not tiled, consider using a tile baseboard instead of wood. If you have small children who enjoy splashing in the tub or if your bathroom is such that step-ping in and out of the tub is likely to create splashes along the wall, the tile will provide the extra waterproofing you need.

HOMEOWNER TIP

There Is No Such Thing as a Simple Bathroom

I made the mistake of thinking remodeling a bathroom would be a "little" project. It was a downstairs bath that didn't need to be used reg-ularly, and I didn't think I would mind having people in and out of my house for a few weeks. I was wrong.

• Bathroom remodeling is dirty! Watch the dust fly when they demolish the tile.

• Bathrooms require an enormous amount of work from a large number of people (carpenters, plumbers, electricians, tile-layers). For that reason, the choreogra-phy of scheduling is formidable.

• Because the rest of your house seems so normal, it may be hard-er to tolerate the dust.

I think I'd do an entire addition before I took on another bathroom!

- ☐ If you have young boys in the house, create at least four feet of tile wainscoting around the toilet. It will make cleaning and maintenance much easier.
- ☐ Traditional toilets were constructed in two parts with the water tank and toilet bowl separate. More modern one-piece toilets are easier to clean and are particularly helpful for those who have young boys.
- ☐ Any electrical outlets near the sink or tub should be Ground Fault Circuit Interrupters (GFCI). Be sure to put an outlet near the mirror.
- ☐ The lighting in a bathroom needs to be first-rate. Plan for ambient lighting (perhaps a ceiling fixture) as well as a light on both sides of the mirror so that you won't have shadows while applying makeup.

Garage

If you're adding a garage, consider adding another 4 to 6 feet of space at the front and have it sectioned off as a separate work room. Doing so provides you with extra space at minimal cost. Some people use it for storage; others turn it into a workshop.

- ☐ Design the garage windows in places that induce cross-ventilation, particularly if it will be used for hobbies.
- ☐ If you've got space above your garage, add pull-down stairs and ask that they build some "attic" space for additional storage.
- ☐ Have a drain built into the floor for easy cleaning.

Finishing Touches

- ☐ Paint first or carpet first? You can argue this either way, however, a strong case can be made for getting the painter in first. Getting a paint spill out of a carpet is going to be far more difficult than having a painter come back to touch-up any nicks that occur when the carpet is laid.
- ☐ Tell your painter to put a coat of polyurethane paint on all your closet shelves. It will greatly simplify cleaning.
- ☐ Create a "What I Learned" sheet to sum up good ideas that you heard about or thought of after you were finished with this project. You'll be even smarter the next time!

Chapter 5

The While-ya's and Honey-do's

"The best renovation experiences we've had are those where we have planned every detail we could think of in advance," says Sam Miller, the owner of a 110-year-old home that has been renovated in stages. "Our kitchen renovation was a good example. When planning it, we also walked through the entire house thinking of what else needed to be done.

"When we put our plans out to bid, we asked that a few projects be priced separately. Later we eliminated items for cost reasons, but we did get some of the additional work done. Planning on these extras helped us prepare for construction, since we knew in advance what other parts of the house would be involved. I assume it also helps the contractor because he can plan out everything at the same time."

By taking this approach, the Miller family avoided as much of the unexpected as possible and managed their remodeling dollar—and their time—in the best way possible.

Most homeowners tackle a basic project, and then once the crew is on site come up with what are sometimes referred to as "while-ya's" (While you're here, could you . . .) and "honey-do's" (Honey, could you do . . .). These are the projects that you want to get done while the household is being torn up anyway.

The homeowner's intent is correct. There's no better time to catch up with maintenance—an important aspect of safeguarding your home investment. The problem is that while-ya's and honey-do's can slow down a job and increase your expenses, often in a way that exceeds what you would have paid had you committed to the other aspects of the project in advance. No doubt about it, last-minute extras blow a budget.

In this chapter, we'll outline some of the tasks that frequently appear as while-ya's and honey-do's, and help you think through what other household projects make sense to do now. Cost will limit your ultimate list, but this process provides you with the opportunity to set priorities on the extras you undertake.

So What Exactly Are While-ya's?

While-ya's are extra remodeling projects that make sense now. They include anything from wiring your house for a stereo or replacing old insulation to redoing a hall closet or an extra bathroom. Basically, while-ya's fall into two categories:

Tasks that are convenient to do because certain walls are already open. The Miller family had an aging bathroom above their kitchen. While they didn't want to spend the money to completely remodel the bathroom at the same time they were doing the kitchen, they did plan for the workers to replace the old pipes as long as the walls were open, a task that was simple and affordable since the pipes were exposed anyway. A few years later when they were ready to do the upper floor bathroom, a lot of the new piping was already in place because they had done it earlier. If walls are open, old pipes are worth replacing in any case. It isn't costly if done then, and it's the best insurance against having to replace burst or deteriorating pipes at a later date.

Additional renovation projects that make sense to do because you have a crew of workers there anyway. These items are the affordable add-ons. When the Davis family in Portland renovated a bathroom, it was adjacent to their master bedroom closet, so they had it rebuilt at the same time. Either project could have been done independently, but as long as the area was under construction it made sense to do both at once. (You needn't limit yourself to projects in adjacent rooms if you don't mind another area of your home being torn up.)

And What about Those Honey-do's?

Honey-do's are tasks that fall into the home handyman category such as, the damage from the leak that showed up during the winter, the robe hook you'd like put up in the bathroom, the new knobs you'd like put on the exterior doors, the basement pump you'd like to have repaired. The possibilities are endless. Keep in mind that some honey-do's are quite complex. If a honey-do is the result of some type of damage, there are three steps to this task: First the original problem (a leak?) must be taken care of; next, someone must diagnose that the original cause of the problem has been fully repaired (this may involve pulling up floor boards, crawling through the attic, or having someone climb on the roof); only then can you take the final step and make the cosmetic repairs.

Honey-do's can also be deceptive. Most seem like simple tasks, but even ten-minute tasks can add up to a good many hours. What's more, if you've ever started a "little project," you know that if one small thing goes wrong, it can take several hours to solve. Despite appearances, these aren't always simple chores.

Identifying the While-ya's and Honey-do's

Notebook in hand, inspect your house inside and out, listing everything you can that would put your home in excellent repair. Also write down the future remodeling projects you might like to do. Perhaps you want to do one bathroom now, but later on you may want to do the other. You can always decide not to do these jobs, but anticipating them now will give you the best shot at getting the job done at the best price.

CONTRACTOR TIP

We're Happy to Do While-ya's and Honey-do's When . . .

If while-ya's and honey-do's are on the initial list of items on which a contractor bids, you'll get a better price. If the contractor knows in advance, he can plan for supplies, and he knows that while the plumber is there on the main job he can cross over and help with one of the honey-do's. It's an efficient use of contractor time and a better use of your money.

Your schedule is another reason to plan ahead. We are frequently asked to do these extras while on the job, and in addition to the unplanned expense, homeowners fail to realize that it will extend our overall project time. So when you think about saying, "While you're here, could you just . . .", remember that it's going to take longer and cost more. That's why it pays to plan ahead.

Here's what I explain to my clients (and it's in my contract with them).

1. If I find a rotten beam when I am working, I take care of it, without question. But if, in the middle of the job, you ask me to drywall the basement "while you're here doing the kitchen," I have the right to say "no." I may have booked my next job, and if I do your while-ya I may not be able to keep the promise I kept to the next client, something you wouldn't like if it were you. However, if I can do it and the job is reasonable, I will do it.

2. I have the right to charge for it. Whether it's fixing a gutter, putting up a closet pole, or refinishing your basement, I can't do every add-on without extra pay. (Most homeowners get a few "freebies" thrown in, but as any businessperson knows, we can't do a lot of extras for free.)

How your additional projects would be categorized (while-ya or honey-do) depends on what your "core" project is, so here is a list of possible while-ya's and honey-do's:

Exterior and mechanical:

- Walk along the foundation of your home, (from the inside, too) looking for excessive cracks and deterioration.
- Check for termites by watching for small, vertical mud tunnels on the inside or outside of foundation walls. (The solution here will be provided by an exterminator; however, damage repair would involve a contractor.)
- Do you need to do asbestos or lead abatement? Consult chapter 8.
- Check your drainage system. Are your leaders and gutters clear? If you have a sump pump, is it working properly?
- If no one has been on your roof for a time, you might have it checked. Replace or repair any loose, torn, or corroded shingles or flashing. (Moisture trapped under a loose shingle can eventually cause extensive damage.) The chimney should be examined at the same time.
- Check decks and porches. Is flooring sound? Are steps and railings in good shape?
- Will any part of the yard be torn up due to construction? Would that simplify adding a sprinkler system?
- Do you need new sidewalks or does the driveway need resurfacing?
- How is the exterior finish of your home (paint, stucco, siding)? Is any of the exterior paint blistering or peeling? This problem can spread if not corrected. If you are putting on an addition where they will be matching exterior work, hiring workers to freshen up the rest of it makes a lot of sense.
- Have you always wanted to install air conditioning?
- Have you intended to put in an attic fan?
- Do you need a larger capacity water heater?
- How is the energy efficiency of your home? Do you need new weather stripping? Are your pipes and hot-water heater insulated?
- Have you intended to convert your furnace from oil to gas?
- Do you need to upgrade your appliances? The energy savings of some of the new appliances are considerable: An old refrigerator can cost as much as $150 in electrical usage while more energy-efficient models use as little as $30–$50. Dishwashers, washing machines, and dryers can all realize savings too.
- Once you have a crew on site, ask that the insulation be checked. Adding new where the old has deteriorated can make a difference in summer and winter.

- Evaluate the age of your furnace. Old models aren't as efficient.
- Investigate adding an electrostatic air cleaner to your HVAC (heating, ventilation, and air conditioning) system. These devices trap particles of pollen, dust, asbestos, fibers, bacteria, and other matter that float through your house. They need to be cleaned frequently, particularly in the early months following construction.

Interior:

- Are any unaffected rooms in need of a paint job?
- Check ceilings for leaks (you'll notice a circular stain if water is coming through).
- Check stairs and railing.
- How is the caulking and the tile in existing baths and the kitchen?
- Do parts of the house show shoddy workmanship?

Some while-ya's can contribute to a comfortable lifestyle. Consider the following:

- Stereo wiring that puts sound into several rooms.
- A household intercom system. No more kids screaming, "DAAAAAD! The phone's for you!"
- Additional doorbell chimes, particularly if the house is being expanded.
- Towel warmer.
- Skylight.
- Additional telephone wire. Ask the workers to put in wiring for multiple lines. Homes of the future will have modems and faxes and additional regular lines. Wiring now will save money later.
- Central vacuum system. This enables you to go from room to room with a hose and the necessary attachments; in each room there is a "hose plug" that sucks all the dust and dirt into a central receptacle in the basement.

A Recommended While-ya

If you tackle only one while-ya, let it be upgrading your electrical system. This is no job for your brother-in-law. Electrical wiring can be deadly to work with, and, if done improperly and not to code, it can be a serious fire hazard. (There have been situations where homes have suffered fire damage because of illegal wiring, and they were not covered

---

INSIDER'S TIP

Windows and More Windows

What condition are the windows in? Do they stick? Are any broken? Do they let in winter drafts? Are you missing screens or storm windows? You may want to talk to your contractor about pricing replacement windows (thermal double-glazed windows work well and are energy efficient but they are costly) or repairing the old.

Repairing can be less expensive in the short run, but old windows are old windows; you'll be repairing them again before too long. Old single-pane windows also account for 20% to 50% of heat loss, so ultimately some of your replacement cost is made up in energy savings. Once you get some prices and compare the features, you'll be prepared to make a decision.

---

by insurance because the work was not done according to the electrical code.)

If you still have a fuse-based electrical system, you may want to upgrade to a circuit breaker box. One advantage to circuit breakers is that when a breaker trips, the homeowner simply resets it—some systems have a "trip indicator" so that you will immediately know which one was affected.

While you can manage your household electricity by watching how many appliances and lights you put on each circuit, you still run the risk of blowing a circuit by using the microwave when the mixer is on, or you may lose everything on your computer if your daughter plugs her hair dryer into the same circuit.

In new buildings in the United States, one hundred amps has been set as the minimum electrical requirement. (An ampere is the standard unit for measuring the strength of an electric current.) But if you're frequently running air conditioners, power tools, a microwave, hair dryers, or a personal computer, chances are you're on overload. (Frequent tripping of the circuit breaker or blowing of the fuse indicates this.) Many electricians say that a 200-amp panel is best for the home of the future. Today electricians recommend dedicated lines (the plug that services the appliance has nothing else on the line) for computers and for high-amp appliances such as refrigerators and microwaves.

And while you're at it, add outlets. Some homes are built with only one or two outlets per room. While extension cords can solve the immediate problem, they are also a fire hazard. For a little money, you can better equip each room for its necessary appliances.

Please Go through Channels

When it comes to the honey-do's, the homeowner is very likely to simply pull the carpenter aside and say: "Couldn't you just do me a favor . . ."

This is the wrong approach. The carpenter has no expense account for any supplies, and I'm counting on his finishing his work by a certain time. If you waylay him, we can't stay on schedule. If you have extra chores, here's what to do:

• Speak directly to the contractor and ask if there's any way they can fit in time for the work you have in mind.

• If you do ask for permission to have the carpenter help you with a chore, don't give him another eleven things to do after I leave.

• Do expect to be charged for it. While there may be a few things we can throw in for free, there's a limit to the number of handyman chores we can do. One family for whom we did a $250,000 renovation had $110,000 worth of while-ya's and honey-do's!

Remember, too, any outlets in bathrooms, kitchens, pool areas, or garages should be ground fault circuit interrupters (GFCI) for your family's protection. These outlets automatically shut off the power into the outlet if the internal transformer senses a problem.

While talking to your contractor, ask about a secondary surge arrester. It will protect your home from power surges that can damage many of today's electrical appliances.

Electrical upgrades can generally be done in a couple of days and will definitely not be the most expensive while-ya you undertake. Unless you're in a new home or one that has recently been rewired, this is perhaps the wisest investment you can make.

A While-ya for the Next Millennium

In only a few years, families are likely to have a computer for the kids in the family room and at least one additional terminal for the adults. Buying and "loading" each computer with all the necessary accessories is a costly proposal. People who are building new homes or renovating are starting to create the technical environment that would permit them to link their computers to save money on all the peripherals.

If you're extending the house or gutting a room, consider running the wires that you'll need for such a system. Call in a computer consultant for advice. (While you're at it, add extra phone wires for the modems that will undoubtedly be added as well.) If you're not certain of your needs and don't want to have wires run now, have a plumber run a 1.5-inch pipe from basement to attic. Later on, all manner of computer network and cable TV wires can be run through this "chase" with minimum hassle.

This while-ya will prepare your house for a future in which you'll enjoy such technological luxuries as needing only one printer to service the entire household, and rather than upgrading several individual machines, the home's central processing unit will handle everything because its memory will be almost limitless.

Some Typical While-yas: Cost and Time

While prices vary throughout the country, these are some general costs for the following while-ya's.

While-ya	Price	Time
Upgrade electrical to 200 amps	$1500.00	2 days
Add insulation around large family room	$.50–$1.00/sq. foot 15' × 20' family room,ceiling, and floor: $600.00	1–2 days
New aluminum gutters and leaders on 2500 sq. foot house	$750.00	less than a day
New h/c water pipes in open walls	$500.00	1 day

What to Do about Asbestos and Lead

If the workers of yesterday knew what we know now about construction materials like asbestos and lead-based paint, they could have saved us a lot of time and angst! As it is, homeowners of today are faced with some difficult dilemmas regarding how to safeguard their families' health.

Although information on these topics changes regularly with new studies and new opinions, the following is what we can currently tell you about two substances in the home that are sometimes disturbed during remodeling: asbestos and lead-based paint.

Asbestos

Asbestos is a naturally occurring substance that can be inhaled simply by strolling through the great outdoors. The California state rock, the serpentine, is a prime source of asbestos. Before it came into disrepute, asbestos was one of the most-trusted forms of building material. Once valued for its durability and heat resistance, asbestos was widely used in insulation, floor tiles, and roofing in homes built prior to the 1970s.

Millions of us grew up under asbestos ceilings and above asbestos floor tiles, and many older homes had heating pipes wrapped in asbestos. There is no scientific certainty that a home's asbestos has been fatal to its occupants.

However, in the 1970s the federal government established a link between the fibrous mineral and severe respiratory diseases, including lung cancer. Those affected were primarily unprotected industrial work-ers who made their livings working with or around the substance. As a result of these findings, the government began limiting some of its most dangerous applications, and a widespread movement to remove asbestos from homes and businesses began.

Although many people have taken steps to remove asbestos from their homes, some experts now feel that it may be just as safe to encapsulate it. Asbestos materials are safe when intact, but when broken or pulverized they release fibers that are hazardous when inhaled. The act of removing it may actually release more fibers into the air than is necessary.

However, because home remodeling involves cutting through and breaking down surfaces, this is an important time to determine whether or not your home has any asbestos, where it is located, and whether it will be affected during remodeling.

The best way to make this evaluation is to consult with your contrac-tor or to call in an expert. Get a referral from the contractor or from someone who knows a reputable company. If you locate an expert by looking under "Asbestos Removal" in the Yellow Pages, don't let them do any work until you've checked their references.

As you go through your home, keep in mind that newer products will not contain asbestos. Look closely at the following areas:

- Steam pipes, boilers, and furnace ducts that may be insulated with asbestos.
- Pre-1978 resilient floor tiles (vinyl, asbestos, asphalt, and rubber) and their backings.
- Cement sheet, millboard, and paper used as insulation around furnaces and wood-burning stoves.
- Door gaskets in furnaces, wood stoves, and coal stoves.
- Sound-proofing or decorative material sprayed on walls and ceilings.

- Patching and joint compounds for walls and ceilings and textured paints.
- Asbestos cement roofing, shingles, and siding.

If you have any doubts about whether or not something contains asbestos, there are special labs that will test samples for you for about $25 to $35. Look under "Asbestos Labs" in the Yellow Pages and call for information on how to remove a sample. As you remove it, spray down the area with water to reduce the release of airborne fibers.

If your renovation will involve disturbing these areas for cosmetic reasons, for repair work, or to tie together old and new systems in the house, then you should have the asbestos taken care of in advance by specialists.

An alternative to removal is encapsulating the material. Discuss this possibility with the experts. It can be less expensive than removal, but, if the asbestos may be disturbed later by a burst pipe or the need to repair something, you may be well advised to have it taken out.

An advantage to removal is that potential buyers these days often insist that any home they purchase have all asbestos sealed over or professionally removed.

Hire a well-recommended professional to handle the removal or encapsulation for you. They will seal off the area involved and remove any household belongings, and they should perform a complete cleanup afterwards. No sweeping, vacuuming, or dusting should be done until they are completely finished with their work. It will simply put more fibers in the air.

Following removal, an air sample should be taken and the report sent directly to the homeowner.

Asbestos needn't be a major concern to you now or during renovation so long as you locate where it is in your home and, in consultation with an expert, make a conscious decision as to how to handle it.

Lead-Based Paint

Lead is a toxic substance that is practically unavoidable. It is found in water, soil, and certain ceramic dishes, and especially in the lead-painted walls, window frames, doors, and moldings of an estimated 57 million homes in the United States.

Lead was once prized as a bonding agent for paint and was valued as a paint additive for many reasons. For exterior work, it was particularly resistant to damage from sunlight, and it was so toxic that mildew would not grow on it. For interior work it was simply more durable. Lead in paint was a selling point from the early years of this century until 1978 when it was discovered that it was hazardous, and it was finally banned.

The dust and chips from lead-based paint are dangerous when swallowed or inhaled. The smallest lead dust particles cannot be seen but they can get into the body and are particularly dangerous to young children and pregnant women. Lead can affect children's developing nervous systems, causing reduced IQ and learning disabilities. Adults are not as susceptible, but those who show high lead levels may notice symptoms varying from headaches to high blood pressure and a long list of other possible symptoms.

If you live in a home built before 1978, there is a high probability that there is some lead in your home, possibly in the paint or in the soldered pipe joints.

Homeowners are going to be made more aware of the lead issue some time in 1996 when a federal disclosure law, The Residential Lead-Based Paint Hazard Reduction Act, is expected to go into effect. This law will require every home seller to disclose the presence of any known lead-based hazards in residences built before 1978, the year the federal government banned the use of lead as an additive to paint for residential use. The buyers must be given a lead-hazard information pamphlet before the sales agreement is signed, and they will have ten days from the time of the signing to have the home inspected. If lead-based paint is discovered, the buyers would be able to cancel the contract or factor potential lead-removal costs into the purchase price of the home.

Remodeling is a time to be particularly careful about lead levels in the home. When work is done to these surfaces or walls are taken down, the likelihood of lead particles being released is high. Even if the original paint has been covered with new paint or another covering, cracked or chipped painted surfaces can expose the older, lead-based paint layers, possibly creating a lead hazard.

Before worrying about lead and remodeling, you must first determine whether you have a lead problem in your house and, if so, on what surfaces. To accomplish this, you'll need professional help. To find a lead inspector, contact your local health department or call the National Lead Information Center Clearinghouse at (800) 424-LEAD. (Do-it-yourself kits are available but government officials question their accuracy.)

Testing for lead formerly involved removing chips of paint from numerous surfaces—sometimes as many as 150—and having them evaluated at a laboratory. This was laborious and expensive (as much as $4,000). Now most inspectors will test the surfaces of your home by using a portable X-ray fluorescence (XRF) machine, which measures the amount of lead in the paint. Charges are generally $300–$500.

If lead-based paint is found, consider the surfaces that have been identified as having a high content. If doors are the primary culprit, they can be removed and sent out to be stripped. Window sashes can be removed and a stripping solution can be used to remove the paint.

If the problem is more pervasive, have the removal or encapsulation done by a worker who has been trained to protect your family and home from exposure. The person who inspected your home may run such a service or will know someone who does. If you want to get other names for price comparison, consult your local health department again, or check the Yellow Pages under "Lead." When you speak to the lead abatement services ask for several references and ask if they have taken an EPA-accredited course on safe and proper procedures for lead removal.

After testing your home but before having any work performed, have young children take a blood test. According to the EPA, one out of every six preschoolers suffers from lead poisoning. (Children under the age of six are most vulnerable.) If their blood content is high beforehand, your pediatrician may recommend that they live elsewhere during the remodeling.

Although all of this may be somewhat alarming, the good news about renovation is that by taking some action you may actually make things better. If you have a high content of lead-based paint in the house, then every time you open an old window or a cabinet you may be stirring up levels of lead dust that endanger your family.

If you've hired a specially trained contractor to manage your lead problem, he will proceed in much the same way that an asbestos removal company would. If the paint is to be removed, all furniture, rugs, and draperies will be removed from the area. Any surfaces, such as a kitchen counter, will be covered and taped with heavy plastic, and refrigerator seals will be covered and taped to prevent food contamination.

Most removal methods involve wetting all work surfaces to minimize dust, and a chemical "peel away" substance is used to remove the lead paint. The paint should not be scraped or sandblasted because doing so only releases lead dust into the air.

If they are working outside, the soil should be covered with a plastic tarp to prevent contamination. After closing all windows, ask that the workers seal them with plastic on the inside to further prevent contamination.

Cleanup should be with a HEPA (high-efficiency particulate air) filter-equipped vacuum cleaner that can remove small lead particles from floors, window sills, and carpets and will keep particles inside the vacuum cleaner instead of blowing them back out into the air the way a normal vacuum does.

If the specialists recommend covering the trouble spots, they will use an encapsulant, which is a heavy, plasterlike substance that is painted on and then hardens. This is considered effective for approximately ten years, and it's about 25% cheaper than removal. The lead abatement services are best equipped to do this as the wall must be primed and the super-sticky encapsulant requires special handling.

While the work is taking place, be sure that all heating and air-conditioning systems are turned off so that the dust is not blown through the home. In addition, keep nonworkers, particularly children and pregnant women, away from the work area.

While there should be no reason for you to be cleaning up, if per-chance you are doing so, the only household detergent effective at cleaning up lead dust is powdered high phosphate automatic dishwash-er detergent. Lead-specific cleaning products are also available at some paint and hardware stores.

At the conclusion of the process, areas should be tested for lead dust contamination after the final cleanup. The report should be sent direct-ly to the homeowner.

Protecting children against lead poisoning is not yet a perfected sci-ence. Some young children live through renovations without a problem, others show high levels of lead even when all precautions have been taken. One additional measure that may help is seeing that your child eats regular, nutritious meals (more lead is absorbed on an empty stom-ach). Make certain that your child's diet contains plenty of iron (found in liver, fortified cereal, cooked beans, spinach, and raisins) and calcium (milk, yogurt, cheese, and cooked greens).

Because remodeling is certainly not the only cause for high lead lev-els in children, many experts are pushing for all children under the age of six to be tested every year. Lead poisoning can be treated if it's found early.

Understanding Lead Levels

If your child should have slightly elevated blood levels, talk to your pediatrician. Recent research seems to indicate that for lead exposure to cause permanent damage, it must be over an extended period of time. So, by following the recommendations of your doctor, you should be able to prevent your child from suffering any permanent ill effects.

According to the Center for Disease Control and Prevention in Atlanta, here's how to respond to elevated lead-level readings:

10–14 micrograms of lead per deciliter of blood. No action necessary. Retest child within a couple of months.

15–19 micrograms. Doctors are told to educate parents on how to clean up household dust that might contain lead. Parents are also told to encourage children to eat food rich in iron and calcium, which helps prevent the absorption of lead. If elevated levels persist after retesting in a few months, a professional inspector should be called in to identify the source.

20 micrograms and above. Immediately identify and eliminate the source of lead in the home by encapsulating it or having it removed.

45 micrograms and above. Medical intervention may be necessary. One treatment, chelation, a pharmacological therapy, is administered orally or intravenously and draws lead out of the blood.

See the resource section for a listing of agencies that provide more information on lead.

Homeowner Checklist

- Consider other possible remodeling projects that might be taken on at this time.
- Walk through your home and around the outside of it. Are there repairs that should be done?
- Seriously consider upgrading your electrical system.
- If you need more information, do the research. (What will window replacement cost? What kind of in-wall computer wiring would be helpful?)
- Select the items you might like to have taken care of at this time and add them to your list of bid items. If these extras are priced separately, you can always decide not to do them.

Chapter 6

Serious Business: Selecting a Contractor

"Couldn't I be my own contractor and save a little money?" you may be thinking. Many people who try this end up paying more—they make mistakes in materials that a pro would know to avoid, or it costs them because the tradespeople put amateurs pretty far down on the list. After you read what a good contractor will do for you, you'll likely be more than happy to find those who are reputable.

This is the most important chapter of the book. If you do your homework and hire wisely, you can rest easy. If you don't, you could be entering into one of the most unpleasant experiences of your life. Do your research, check references, and trust your instincts.

What Is a Contractor?

The term contractor generally refers to what's known as a general contractor, sometimes called a remodeler or builder. (You will also hear of tile contractors, roofing contractors, and swimming pool contractors, to name a few, but these businesspeople oversee only the work specified in their titles.)

In home remodeling a general contractor is in charge of the overall job, whether it's the entire gutting of a house or the renovation of a small bathroom (which actually requires intricate contractor-lead choreography because so many types of workers, from carpenter and plumber to electrician and tile-layer, must coordinate their work in a single, small space). The contractor sets the work schedule, orders materials, and hires reliable tradespeople (also known as subcontractors or subs): plumbers, electricians, carpenters, roofers, and any other members of the building trades required.

The contractor also oversees the all-important coordination of work and materials. All materials must be on site by the day the workers need it—not too far in advance for fear of damage or theft from the work site, and not too late or everyone waits. And if one tradesperson's job is proceeding more slowly than anticipated, then it is up to the contractor to reschedule all those who follow. Daily occurrences require constant rescheduling.

The contractor is also responsible for inspection of materials, inspection of workmanship performed by the subcontractors, paying bills, coping with changes, and getting the city and county inspections performed at the appropriate time so that at job's end, she can provide you with a new certificate of occupancy. The general contractor should also offer a reasonable guarantee (generally one year) on the work performed.

The Intangible Value of a Home Contractor

"Well, it sounds like the contractor has a lot to do, but I'm here, why can't I do all that myself?" some homeowners say. On a small job, such as a new deck that involves just one type of skilled worker (a carpenter), you certainly could.

Larger jobs require knowledgeable on-site management on a virtually full-time basis. Even if you have the time, you may lack the knowledge to keep the job going smoothly and correctly. Contractors have experience in their favor. Good ones know which brand of insulation is the best; they've seen what happens with certain types of kitchen tile; they've got shortcuts that save time and money without sacrificing quality. A homeowner attempting this supervisory job usually lacks experience, which in turn may mean that the money saved by not hiring a contractor will be quickly eaten up by unexpected costs.

Contractors also have contacts and leverage. He or she knows the best plumber in town, and that same plumber who is too busy to schedule in the homeowner's job may well find time to do the same work for a contractor who has been supplying him with work through the years.

How much will hiring a contractor add to the expense of your job? Contractor's fees are built into the overall bid given on the job. The percentage a contractor factors in as compensation is based on time, job difficulty, convenience, contractor availability, and how the work dovetails with other jobs. Contractors will frequently give better prices on jobs that let them work through the December holidays (a time when most homeowners don't want their homes torn up). The price is also set competitively. In a weak economy when little construction or remodeling work is available, a contractor will add in less profit in order to keep her crews working.

Living through a home renovation is trying at best, and by choosing to use a general contractor you minimize your own difficulties. You do one thorough research job—on what general contractor to use—and after that, you rely on his knowledge and experience to find and use the best materials and to hire good, reliable subcontractors. You're freed of having to worry about small and large problems, such as the tile going up crooked, because if it does, it's the contractor's responsibility to fix it.

You'll also find that good contractors can save you money, partly by knowing where to get the best deal on labor and supplies but also because of their acquired knowledge. He may show up for the first interview in a T-shirt, but in all likelihood he knows his stuff.

Sit down with any good contractor you're giving the plans to, and say, "I want you to point out any places on the plans where we might be able to save time or money." Chances are you'll get some helpful ideas. For instance, you may not realize that the windows specified by the architect must be custom-made; if you switch to a standard-size window you'll save a bundle. A contractor can sometimes recommend a ready-made trim that looks similar to the custom-made trim indicated and that can save even more money. The bids on putting marble in your new bathroom may be higher than you budgeted, but sometimes, a contractor can recommend something that gives a similar look for a lower price.

Coordinating with the architect on any contractor-suggested changes may require tact, but a reasonable professional will listen to the need for additional time- or money-savings and can help you weigh the possible trade-offs.

In some cases, you may say, "I understand about the cost, I've got to have it custom-made," but there will also be areas where you may decide ready-made is good enough.

HOMEOWNER TIP

Benefiting from Their Field Experience

"What would you do if it were your house?" is an important question to pose to the contractor upon occasion. You may decide to go the more costly route, but homeowners ought to at least know about the full range of choices.

When we got our first estimates, we needed to reduce the cost, but like all homeowners, we didn't want to give up anything substantial. We asked Kevin to go over our plans, and he immediately suggested using stock posts on our deck instead of the custom-made ones the architect had designed. There were more than twenty posts, so we saved several thousand dollars by making that change and we saved time. We decided to use the custom-made ones on the front porch and were amazed at the number of days it took a skilled carpenter to build those posts correctly.

How to Find Good Contractors to Bid on Your Job

If you're like most people, you started listening for names of good contractors just as soon as you started contemplating getting work done. (If you're restoring a historic home, you should be listening for contractors with experience in that area.) If you need additional names for your list, the following are some ways to get recommendations.

Personal referral. Your neighbors or friends who have had work done, of course, are the first place to start. People generally love talking about their experiences, so you might even knock on a strange door or two where remodeling has been going on. Here are some questions to ask:

- Who did the work?
- Would you recommend this contractor?
- What was the crew like to have around?
- Was the project on time and on budget? (Most jobs aren't. Even the best workers can run into rotten floorboards or, in a very old home, a beam or pipe not shown or provided for in the plans. This causes delays in timing and will also add to the ultimate cost. Listen to how the homeowner explains any problems that occurred; maybe it was terrible contractor management, or maybe it was a run of bad luck.)

Other tradesmen. If you like your plumber or electrician, ask for a referral. Another worker will know the best contractors in town.

Material suppliers. Stop by your local lumberyard and tell one of the salespeople what type of renovation you're doing. Ask if he will recommend good people to consider for the job.

Realtors. Even if it's been a few years since you bought your house, call the real estate office you purchased it through. Explain what you're doing and ask who they might recommend. Most agents maintain a good list of tradesmen for buyers who are new to the area and need to get work done.

Professional organizations. Both the National Association of Home Builders Remodelers Council and the National Association of the Remodeling Industry maintain lists of contractors by area. Contact them for names and then check references carefully. (See the resource section.)

Asking Contractors to Bid

Of the names gathered, select the contractors from whom you would like to receive bids.

How many estimates should you get? For a smaller job such as building a deck or finishing off a room in the basement, three bids are usually adequate. (With fewer variables, there will likely be less fluctuation in the bids.) For larger projects with more components, five bids should be enough. Getting estimates will be time consuming for you as you must give each group access to your home. It can be costly as well, because each contractor must be given a set of plans. (Architects charge for copies of the plans.)

We've created the following worksheet for you to use as you talk to contractors. Make copies of it so that you can fill out one per contractor. These are the questions you need to cover for each person you're considering for the job. After getting answers to all the questions, attach the appropriate form to the bid submitted by each contractor. This provides you with an organized method for deciding which contractor to use.

Getting in Touch with the Contractors

The first time you get in touch with the contractors, you're calling simply to ascertain each one's interest in your project and his potential availability.

Contractors tend to be on the run all day, so if the ones you are phoning don't have a secretary, answering machine, or service, try calling early in the morning or late in the day. Once the two of you have connected, describe the job, tell the contractor who he was referred by, and suggest what you hope will be the time frame for the job. "Are you interested?" is the next logical question.

Sometimes actually getting a contractor to stop by and give you an estimate is a challenge. If this is the case, and you're finding that you may actually have difficulty getting someone to do the job, you've got to explain your job's appeal. The most appealing thing to any contractor is money, so if you have cash available or financing arranged, let the contractor know. Other good points are also worth mentioning: Are you flexible on timing? (The contractor can do the job during a lull.) Is it winter and the house is empty? (The contractor has a good inside job for his crew for the cold season.) If this is a small job, does it precede a bigger one you'll have him bid on? These types of benefits may help you find the contractor who will eventually devote his resources to you.

If you have copies of the plans ready, set a date for the plans to be picked up. For this initial meeting, ask each contractor to bring along a brochure or photos of some of the projects she has done.

When you first meet, you'll want to get some sense of who this person is and what she is like. Also make it clear what it will be like to work in your home. Point out anything unusual—that, for example, you raise sheepdogs and that the dogs' safety will need to be provided for; or that your baby will soon be crawling, so workers will need to make certain no stray nails or dangerous tools are on the floor in family

---

Contractor name _____ Telephone _____
Company name _____
Address _____

Referred by _____
License number _____ Years in business ____
Estimated cost on job _____
Work and materials guaranteed? _____
Estimated time of completion _____

Current or recent client referrals:
Name _____ Telephone _____
Address _____

Name _____ Telephone _____
Address _____

Name _____ Telephone _____
Address _____

Bank reference _____

Supplier reference _____

Insurance agent _____

Any complaints from:
Licensing Division _____

Better Business Bureau _____

Clients _____
_____
_____

Any good or bad word-of-mouth? _____
_____

Comments: _____
_____
_____

ACORD. CERTIFICATE OF INSURANCE

ISSUE DATE (MM/DD/YY)

PRODUCER	THIS CERTIFICATE IS ISSUED AS A MATTER OF INFORMATION ONLY AND CONFERS NO RIGHTS UPON THE CERTIFICATE HOLDER. THIS CERTIFICATE DOES NOT AMEND, EXTEND OR ALTER THE COVERAGE AFFORDED BY THE POLICIES BELOW.
	COMPANIES AFFORDING COVERAGE
	COMPANY LETTER **A**
INSURED	COMPANY LETTER **B**
	COMPANY LETTER **C**
	COMPANY LETTER **D**
	COMPANY LETTER **E**

COVERAGES

THIS IS TO CERTIFY THAT THE POLICIES OF INSURANCE LISTED BELOW HAVE BEEN ISSUED TO THE INSURED NAMED ABOVE FOR THE POLICY PERIOD INDICATED, NOTWITHSTANDING ANY REQUIREMENT, TERM OR CONDITION OF ANY CONTRACT OR OTHER DOCUMENT WITH RESPECT TO WHICH THIS CERTIFICATE MAY BE ISSUED OR MAY PERTAIN, THE INSURANCE AFFORDED BY THE POLICIES DESCRIBED HEREIN IS SUBJECT TO ALL THE TERMS, EXCLUSIONS AND CONDITIONS OF SUCH POLICIES. LIMITS SHOWN MAY HAVE BEEN REDUCED BY PAID CLAIMS.

CO LTR	TYPE OF INSURANCE	POLICY NUMBER	POLICY EFFECTIVE DATE (MM/DD/YY)	POLICY EXPIRATION DATE (MM/DD/YY)	LIMITS	
	GENERAL LIABILITY				GENERAL AGGREGATE	$
	COMMERCIAL GENERAL LIABILITY				PRODUCTS-COMP/OP AGG.	$
	CLAIMS MADE OCCUR.				PERSONAL & ADV. INJURY	$
	OWNER'S & CONTRACTOR'S PROT.				EACH OCCURRENCE	$
					FIRE DAMAGE (Any one fire)	$
					MED. EXPENSE (Any one person)	$
	AUTOMOBILE LIABILITY				COMBINED SINGLE LIMIT	$
	ANY AUTO					
	ALL OWNED AUTOS				BODILY INJURY (Per person)	$
	SCHEDULED AUTOS					
	HIRED AUTOS				BODILY INJURY (Per accident)	$
	NON-OWNED AUTOS					
	GARAGE LIABILITY					
					PROPERTY DAMAGE	$
	EXCESS LIABILITY				EACH OCCURRENCE	$
	UMBRELLA FORM				AGGREGATE	$
	OTHER THAN UMBRELLA FORM					
	WORKER'S COMPENSATION				STATUTORY LIMITS	
	AND				EACH ACCIDENT	$
	EMPLOYERS' LIABILITY				DISEASE—POLICY LIMIT	$
					DISEASE—EACH EMPLOYEE	$
	OTHER					

DESCRIPTION OF OPERATIONS/LOCATIONS/VEHICLES/SPECIAL ITEMS

CERTIFICATE HOLDER	CANCELLATION
	SHOULD ANY OF THE ABOVE DESCRIBED POLICIES BE CANCELLED BEFORE THE EXPIRATION DATE THEREOF, THE ISSUING COMPANY WILL ENDEAVOR TO MAIL _____ DAYS WRITTEN NOTICE TO THE CERTIFICATE HOLDER NAMED TO THE LEFT, BUT FAILURE TO MAIL SUCH NOTICE SHALL IMPOSE NO OBLIGATION OR LIABILITY OF ANY KIND UPON THE COMPANY, ITS AGENTS OR REPRESENTATIVES.
	AUTHORIZED REPRESENTATIVE

ACORD 25-S (7/90)   ©ACORD CORPORATION 1990

areas at night. If the contractor dislikes some aspect of the job presented, it's better for both of you to learn it now.

At that meeting you should do these things:

1. Ask if the contractor is licensed and insured.
   * Ask that the contractor mail you a copy of his license—some
     licenses are too large to carry conveniently. When you receive it,
     verify that the license name agrees with the business name he
     presently uses. Also note the address on the license. Remember,
     licensing is important, but not to the exclusion of checking refer-
     ences. (A sample certificate of insurance can be found on page 77.)
   * Ask to see proof of insurance. The contractor should carry **gen-
     eral liability insurance** (covers damages caused to you, your
     family, your property or your neighbors during the course of
     work), **workers' compensation insurance** (covers bodily
     injury to the contractor and his workers; check for an expiration
     date and a monetary amount), and an insurance policy that cov-
     ers the job materials both on site and while in transit. Make a
     note of the insurance carrier. Contractors have been known to
     cancel a policy after getting the job.
2. Find out how long he has been in business and what similar jobs
   each can tell you about.
3. Ask if he belongs to any trade associations. (The National
   Association of the Remodeling Industry or the National Association
   of Home Builders Remodelers Council are two of the major ones.)
   Although membership does not indicate specific qualifications, it
   does tell you that the contractor is serious enough about the profession that he has taken the time to affiliate himself with a professional organization.
4. Find out how your job fits into the contractor's work schedule.

HOMEOWNER TIP

The Schedule

For most homeowners, the timing of the work is important. But
remember, more important than
the start date is the finish date.
Lots of contractors will bring in
some equipment on a day that you
specify, but what a homeowner
really wants to know is when the
equipment will be gone. Instead of
asking, "When can you start?" ask,
"I'd like to have this work finished
by (blank). Do you think you could
have it completed by then?"

Bid Page Example

Jones Residence   Contractor _____

Base Bid

1) General Conditions   _____
2) Sitework/Excavation   _____
3) Concrete Work   _____
4) Masonry   _____
5) Framing   _____
6) Insulation   _____
7) Stucco/Siding   _____
8) Roofing, Gutters, etc.   _____
9) Doors and Hardware   _____
10) Windows   _____
11) Drywall, Taping, etc.   _____
12) Finish Carpentry   _____
13) Ceramic Tile   _____
14) Plumbing   _____
15) Heating   _____
16) Electrical   _____
17) Other   _____
18) Total Base Bid   _____

Can start work by _____
Work will take _____weeks

Present each contractor with the plans. Most will need to spend time at your house (generally at a later date) going over details.

Most homeowners assume that the bidding process involves the contractor walking through the home and giving a rough estimate "the maximum he thinks you'll have to pay . . ." Actually the bidding process is a careful science. Simple jobs (those without a lot of technical or personal detail) may be bid on a square-foot basis, but most bids are carefully prepared using a bid sheet that is similar to the one that follows. Everything, from what the plumber will charge to the contractor (the plumber may need to visit your home) to the cost of tying the new addition into the old house, must be carefully figured. It's a time-consuming process.

Give a deadline for bids so that you've put them on notice that the job will proceed with or without them. You probably won't get all the bids in on time and some leniency is usually necessary. However, by setting a target date, you establish a time when you or your architect can start making follow-up phone calls to any contractors you particularly liked and who you have not yet received a bid from.

As discussed in chapter 3, the more complete and specific your plans (or the more detailed your list of projects to be undertaken), the better off you'll be, especially when getting estimates. If the plans call for a new boiler and the make and model number are specified, then all the bids should factor in the same costs for boiler replacement.

What to Do while You Wait

With your list of five potential contractors in hand, call both the licensing office for your county (often within the Department of Consumer Affairs or the Consumer Protection Office) and the Better Business Bureau. Most consumer affairs departments will tell you by phone if the builder has an up-to-date license and how long she has had it.

While you've got them on the phone, ask about licensing requirements in your area. Licensing requirements vary from state to state (a few states don't require a license) and even city to city. Ask what the minimum standards are for getting a general contractor's license. Some counties require a fee and proof of insurance. The contractor is often required to fill out a form that provides more detailed business information. A few states require that a contractor pass a test demonstrating knowledge of the trades; for example, California requires that contractors spend four years in an apprenticeship prior to getting a license.

Bonding is required in some states. The purpose of bonding is to protect you against substandard work that does not comply with local building codes. There may be a payout feature to cover consumer

---

INSIDER'S TIP

Uncle Harry's Contractor

Yes, even if he did some good work for Uncle Harry you should check out the contractor out and make sure he's legitimate; it may be *your* $25,000 that goes south when he discovers he's in so much debt that he's got to leave town.

If you want to request information concerning complaints from the licensing agency, the request often needs to be in writing. You may want to decide which workers are the strongest contenders for your job before going to the trouble of drafting letters.

INSIDER'S TIP

Check for Complaints

Before starting out, take the time to be certain there are no skeletons in the contractor's past. The Department of Consumer Affairs (or comparable licensing office) is the place to begin because this agency often has the ability to act on complaints filed with them. The action taken may involve mediating a disagreement or taking legal action against a contractor who operates with no license or who takes the money and runs.

What if there are complaints? If you liked the contractor, offer him or her the opportunity to explain. Maybe it was the customer who was difficult. Proceed cautiously though, and check references carefully—you have been forewarned.

expenses if a job has to be redone. However, this fund generally does not kick in when a contractor walks off a job.

Never work with an unlicensed or uninsured contractor. Although licensing isn't a seal of approval, it does indicate that a contractor has taken the initial steps to run a legitimate operation. An unlicensed contractor is usually an uninsured contractor, and this can leave the homeowner open to major financial trouble if there should be an injury or something is damaged during construction.

As the Bid Comes in

Before the deadline, you or your architect should make follow-up phone calls to remind bidders of the approaching date. As you get the estimates, you'll see a wide variety of bid presentations. Some will be extremely detailed, others will be sketchy. In general, the more detailed the bid the less room there is for surprises once work gets underway.

Check through the bids and make sure you are comparing apples to apples. Did each contractor include the specified brand of sink? What about the allowance on hardware? Is it about the same? What about the brand and type of air-conditioning unit that is included? Compare any "allowances" for homeowner-selected items. Are all allowances similar in range? You want to make certain that all prices are based on the same factors.

If the information you have given the contractors has been specific and consistent, then the bids should be within 10% to 15% of each other. If they vary more than that, be suspicious. Some aspect of the plans may have been misinterpreted or it may show a lack of knowledge on the part of the contractor.

If one or two of the bids are off but you particularly liked the contractor, express your desire to work with him and ask if he'll refigure the job with some suggestions on how to bring down costs. If the bid is close but not ideal, there may still be a way to hire the contractor you favor.

If all of the bids are significantly over budget, the problem likely lies with the plans. Talk to the architect about making adjustments so that the renovation is within an appropriate price range.

Time and Materials

Occasionally, a contractor will propose working with you on a **time-and-materials basis**. This is an arrangement in which the client is billed for goods and services, as well as a known markup for the contractor. This arrangement is used sometimes if the plans are vague or if the house is in great disrepair, because in both cases it is difficult for the contractor to estimate the problems that will occur.

This type of arrangement can be a positive or a negative experience for the homeowner. It helps to know the contractor and to feel he is totally trustworthy. It also helps if you're in a situation to supervise occasionally to be certain that "time" doesn't refer to lunchtime, and that "materials" isn't enough windows for three houses.

Under certain circumstances you may actually save money. Sometimes vague plans or a ramshackle house can bring out extraordinarily high bids because no one wants to touch it unless they'll earn a lot of money. Time and materials can actually realize savings.

If you select this method, you're going to have to hold a tight rein on your own desires as well as that of your architect or designer. Without a firm bid to work against, a dreamer who continues to dream can quickly run up the overall expense.

Narrowing the Field

With luck, the bids have helped you narrow the field to two or possibly three contractors. At this point, it's vital that you do serious research.

Failing to check references is the biggest mistake you can make. The Better Business Bureau files are bursting with complaints about home contractors, and the best way to assure that your future contractor isn't on a piece of paper in their files is to check references carefully.

From each contractor you are interested in you need:

- Names of at least five and preferably ten current and recent clients. (If you ask for just a few names, you may get Aunt Mary, Uncle Steve, and Cousin Louie.) A full list of ten people, spot-checked at your discretion, will give you a purer, more representative sampling.

- Business references (architects or suppliers); name of bank.
- Address of a job-in-progress you can visit.
- Introduction to the person who will be on site. (Contractors who work on several jobs simultaneously assign a foreman to each project; this person will handle the day-to-day problems, so it's important that you like and respect him.)

Call previous customers or architect references and say: (Blank) is bidding on some work I'm having done. Could you tell me:

- Was she easy to deal with?
- How was the quality of the work?
- Was the job more or less on time?
- Was the contractor or foreman easy to reach and responsive to phone calls?
- Were there many change orders? If there were change orders, ask about the circumstances. (A change order is a signed document between contractor, homeowner, and architect, if architect is still involved, agreeing to a change in the work to be performed for a specific fee. If the contractor starts the job and discovers a rotten beam or unexpected plumbing problems, these would be corrected after the issuing of a change order. A large number of change orders might signify an old house in bad repair or it might indicate a contractor who has misjudged the job.)
- How were the subcontractors (plumbers, electricians, masons, etc.)?
- How did the contractor and crew get along with the family, neighbors, architect?
- Was she good at on-site decisions?
- Was daily cleanup adequate?
- What about the end of the job? Did he come back to finish all the remaining details?
- Did he seem to run an honest business? (Reports of theft from the house during the course of the job, behavior of workers, a continual stream of changing day-laborers, or substitution of materials are potential points that might be raised in answer to this question.)
- Would you hire this contractor again?

Check business references. Ask for a bank reference as well as vendor references. At the bank you want to inquire if it's a well-managed account and if he has an available line of credit (important to the homeowner so that you won't constantly have to forward cash in order for supplies to be delivered). If he doesn't have a line of credit

---

HOMEOWNER TIP

The Importance of Trust

You are putting your home and your family's comfort in the hands of this contractor, so trust and compatibility are two important issues. Did you like the person? Would you enjoy working intensely with her over a prolonged period? Make certain that there is high personal rapport.

Trust is particularly important because the person you hire will be making decisions every day on your behalf. While they will include you on major items, there are hundreds of details that you need never think about if you hire someone you highly trust.

When we hired Brenner Builders to do our addition, Kevin took my husband to visit several homes in which Kevin had done the remodeling. Their visiting occurred early one Sunday morning. At one home, a key was left under the mat for Kevin to bring George through while the family slept. Though certainly an unexpected situation, it said one thing to us: "These people liked and trusted Kevin!" That's what you're looking for when you select your contractor.

(which *is* hard to obtain when you're relatively new in business), ask the contractor how he plans to manage cash flow so that materials are paid for on time without your help.

Vendors should be willing to report whether or not the contractor pays his bills. If a bill is unpaid, you may want to ask the contractor about it. It may be the vendor who is difficult.

Visit a work site. Is the site clean (for a work site) and safe? Look for quality of workmanship. There's nothing difficult or technical about this. Get an overall impression of how well built the home seems to be and check details such as matching trim around windows and floor boards. You'll notice if the workmanship is poor or sloppy. You can also inquire if the homeowner was satisfied with the quality of the work.

Schedule one more meeting with the contractor or contractors you're still considering. When you set up the meeting, ask that the foreman attend as well. In the end, the on-site supervisor is the one who can make the experience pleasant or miserable. During this final meeting, ask for any suggestions concerning changes they might recommend in the plans to save time and money.

Check on insurance. If you have not yet seen a copy of their certificate of insurance, do so now. If someone gets hurt on the job or a worker burns down your house while soldering a pipe, you are liable if there is no insurance.

Two other "lifestyle" items that you may want to provide for in the contract should be discussed now.

Use of the telephone. On any job that will last longer than two months, the contractor should arrange for a telephone on premises so that workers don't use yours. Some contractors have cellular phones and use these instead. Make certain that any contractor you're considering is willing to accommodate you on this.

Bathroom facilities. Do you have a basement bathroom that workers can have easy access to? If the renovation is major or if the family is reduced to using only one bathroom, you may want to require the contractor to rent a portable toilet for the duration of the job. You should mention ahead of time that this will be one of your contractual stipulations.

The Final Decision

As you make your final evaluation, consider the following issues.

Price. Although you want a good job at the best price, the lowest bid isn't always the one to take. Some contractors will bid low and then as modifications are made, they'll overcharge to compensate. Others who offer too low a price may not be knowledgeable or may have missed something in the plans.

People in the industry always say: "Hire the contractor with the bid in the middle." His price isn't outrageously high, and he isn't so low that he makes you wonder whether his materials are inferior or he is simply desperate for work. It is definitely worth that extra 5% to 10% if you can find a contractor who is easy to work with, does quality work, and won't charge outrageously at every minor change that occurs.

Quality. Did you like the work you saw? Did the contractor seem to take pride in a job well done?

References. Listen carefully to any negative comments you hear. A few comments may not totally dissuade you, but they are certainly reason to be wary.

Compatibility. What will it be like to have this particular group of people in your house for a few months? Does the contractor seem reasonable or hot-headed? Smart? Available to you by phone? Patient about questions? Do you basically like and trust both contractor and the on-site supervisor?

Once your final decision is made, the next step is the contract. Before you proceed, take the time (or ask your architect to do so) to let the others know you've decided to hire someone else. Those who have bid on your job may be saving time for your job and notifying them is common courtesy. (You may use one of them for another job one day.)

Checklist for Selecting a Contractor

- Solicit names of three to five contractors.
- Check out contractor licensing requirements by calling the licensing division for your state (usually within the Department of Consumer Affairs).
- Invite contractors to bid.
- Give out plans and a deadline.
- Follow up with your area's licensing division and the Better Business Bureau.
- Call to remind bidders of the impending deadline.
- Once the bids are in, pursue references for the contractors you're most interested in.
- Visit current jobs.
- Meet one last time with the contractors who are under final consideration.
- Start pulling together a contract. Inform those you didn't select.

Chapter 7

The All-Important Contract

Start a remodeling job on a handshake? Not on your life. Once you've selected a contractor, it is vital that you put your agreement in writing. (Many states require that you do.)

The hallmark of a great contract is that it's fair to both sides. Every protection afforded the homeowner should also have a way of covering the contractor. You both are at risk.

The homeowner who undertakes a remodeling job is at risk for occurrences ranging from having their roof off during a major rainstorm to having their kitchen ripped out but not rebuilt because the contractor left town.

For the contractor, it is his livelihood that's at risk. A homeowner who reneges on promised payments can put a contractor out of business, or the family can make a job so difficult with unreasonable demands and unexpected add-ons that the contractor loses money on the job, a circumstance that occurs more frequently than you might expect.

In a study undertaken by the American Homeowners Foundation (AHF), the organization learned that the bulk of problems that develop between homeowner and contractor arose not from disputes over the contract but because of misunderstandings about items that were not addressed—either verbally or in writing.

"It's amazing the number of major remodeling agreements that are based only on a one-page bid sheet or a handshake," says AHF President Bruce N. Hahn. "No one-page document can cover all elements of a good agreement or even most of the potential problems."

A good written agreement will give you control over your money and your house. Items as simple as completion milestones and the payment schedule provide you with some checkpoints that will help keep the job on track.

If you're just adding a deck, then a simple letter of agreement may suffice. For a more complex project, your architect or contractor likely

---

CONTRACTOR TIP

A Friendly Word about Negotiations

For both parties, the timing of the contract signing is unfortunate. The homeowner is excited about getting started, and the contractor is thrilled when the "you're hired" call comes in. Then there's the contract. We go from the high of "Let's do this job!" to the low, of "Yes, but what about . . . ?"

By its very nature, the contract negotiating process pits homeowner and contractor against each other. However, we all need the legal protection that the contract provides.

Recognize this for what it is—an inevitable interruption in what ought to be a comfortable working relationship. Once the papers are signed, forget any unpleasantness involved in the process. You're partners now. The outcome of the job will depend on cooperation, communication, and to a degree caring. Your contractor is going to take pride in this job, and you should too.

---

has a standard contract that can be amended. For a standard contract form, contact the American Institute of Architects (see the resource section). In addition, the AHF has a form that will help you create a document complete enough to be legally binding.

If your renovation is extensive, then you may want to have an attorney (one with experience in this area) draw up a contract or at least review the one you are going to sign.

Putting together the Contract

Whether you use a boilerplate contract, your own letter of agreement, or a contract form provided by the contractor, what follows are the elements that every contract must have.

Parties Involved.
Homeowner. The contractor needs to have a contract with the owner of the property, so the name here must be the person who holds legal title to your home.

Contractor. The contractor's name, business name, address, telephone number, and license number should all be specified.

Architect or designer. (if she is part of the contract): Name, company name, address, and telephone number should all be listed.

Description of the Work

In short, the contract is for "full and faithful completion of the plans," which are always part of a legal contract.

How much detail you put in the contract depends on the contract documents that will be attached (see the following section, "Enumeration of Contract Documents"). If a complete set of plans and an extensive specifications sheet is part of your attachment, then this paragraph can be short and general, simply referring to these other documents.

Otherwise, as much detail as possible should be spelled out, and, in some cases, the entire remodeling job will be described in a few carefully worded sentences such as these for a home that was to be re-sided:

- Remove existing siding
- Put up new Tyvek
- Attach siding ($1/2$" by 6" beveled Western Red Cedar) with 4" exposure; nailed with stainless steel nails.

Whether the details are provided in the plans, in a separate spec sheet, or in the contract itself, specify everything. No detail is too small. Spell out size, color, model, brand name, and product (Smith Water Heater 2233M). (If you want to give the contractor some leeway, you can insert the words "or approved equivalent.") So don't write "paint," write "two coats of Benjamin Moore." And don't write "install tile," write "install American Olean 4 × 4 glacier white, marble finish."

Either proper plans or the contract should specify what is being provided by the homeowner (or by a separate contractor, such as a cabinetmaker) and what is being provided by the contractor. If this has not yet been carefully thought out, now is the time to make up a list of what each side will provide.

What's Not Included in the Job

This information is as important as the list of what is included. Any part of the project that will be handled by another tradesperson who is paid directly by the homeowner should be specified here. Painting is one aspect of a job that is frequently handled outside the contract.

Unforeseeable problems also are not covered by the contract. If once the kitchen floor is removed it is discovered that there is rotted wood, uneven floors or walls, or an unstable foundation, these issues must be remedied at the owner's expense before continuing.

Enumeration of Contract Documents

This paragraph should list exactly what documents are part of the contract, generally the plans and possibly a specifications sheet or booklet.

Date of Commencement
Upon what date have you agreed that the contractor will begin work?

Date of "Substantial" Completion
This date, of course, is far more relevant than the previous one. Anyone can move a backhoe or a dumpster onto your property on a specific date, but finishing your job by a certain time is another matter. You need to allow time for delays due to bad weather or material that didn't arrive on time.

Duration of the job depends on what's being done. An architect (or the other contractors who bid on the job) or a neighbor who has had similar work done will provide you with a fair idea of how long the job should take. Providing that the contractor doesn't ask for a period much longer than all the rest, then trust that he knows what he's doing on the timing. Home remodeling is not an exact science.

But what is *substantial completion*? This means that the remodeling is complete to the point that it can be occupied for its intended use. Substantial completion is where you may be missing some cabinet doors or a piece of hardware, but you are able to prepare a meal in your almost-complete kitchen.

Contractors will generally request a clause that states that they are not responsible for delays caused by hidden defects or obstacles, Acts of God, strikes, unavailability of labor or materials, or delays caused by owner or his agents/contractors.

Price and Payment Schedule
The full price, which has been agreed upon, should be stated. The payment schedule should include the amount due, and when it is due and payable should be fully spelled out. The best way to stage payments is to tie them to stages of completed work.

The amount of each progress payment must bear a reasonable relationship to the amount of work to be performed, materials to be purchased, or expenses to be incurred.

On a small job, a common arrangement is an initial payment when the work begins, another predetermined amount at the halfway mark, and the balance upon completion. For example, the payment schedule on the siding job described above might be:

- One third payment in advance of starting work
- One third when three sides are completed
- final third upon full completion

For a job that will cost more than $25,000, the upfront payment usually consists of 10% of the total job. The last 10% should be held until the final checklist has been reviewed.

During the negotiation, clarify that payment by check is satisfactory. The cancelled checks will serve as proof of work done for tax purposes.

Homeowner Responsibilities in Preparation for Permit

It is often specified that the owner shall secure and pay for necessary easements, exceptions from zoning requirements, or other actions that must precede the approval of a permit for the project. If owner fails, the contract is void.

Price Variations

This clause is to protect the contractor in case there has been a long delay between the time of his bid and the beginning of the job. The intent of the clause is to hold cost increase of material or labor to 5% and then asks for the right to bill the customer for the difference in price quoted and actual cost of same.

Warranties

Warranties are generally for one year (from date of completion) on labor and materials. There are also extended five-year warranties on structures. Many manufacturers are offering up to ten years on products. Roofing materials are sometimes under warranty for 30 to 40 years.

Specify whether or not the warranty is "full" or "limited." A full warranty means that all faulty products must be repaired or replaced or your money will be returned. A "limited warranty" indicates all replacements and refunds of damaged products are limited in some regard. The name and address of the party who will honor the warranty (contractor, distributor, or manufacturer) must be identified. Clearly identify the time period for the warranty as well.

Proof of Payment

In this business, if the contractor fails to pay the subs or a supplier, the party in question can place a lien against your property to force you to pay them directly (although you may have already paid the contractor for their work). To protect yourself, specify that the contractor provide lien waivers (see sample on page 92) at major stages of completion to verify that the subcontractors and suppliers have been paid. Do not make any final payments to the contractor until you have received those waivers.

How Change Orders Will Be Executed

No job goes entirely according to plan. When they open the walls, they may find rotten wood or rusted pipes that weren't expected or you may decide you want to add more electrical wiring than originally planned.

WAIVER OF LIEN

State of _____ } _____ 19_____

County of _____ } ss.

TO ALL WHOM IT MAY CONCERN:

Whereas _____ the undersigned _____

ha_____ been employed by _____

to furnish _____

_____

for the Building known as _____

City of _____

_____

Lot No. _____ Section _____ Township _____ Range_____

County of _____ State of _____

NOW, THEREFORE, KNOW YE, That _____ the undersigned

for and in consideration of the sum of _____ Dollars

and other good and valuable considerations, the receipt whereof is hereby acknowledged, do hereby waive and release any and all lien, or

claim or right to lien on said above described building and premises under the Statutes of the State of _____

relating to Mechanics' Liens, on account of labor or materials, or both, furnished or which may be furnished, by the undersigned to or on

account of the said _____

_____ for said building or premises.

Given under_____ hand____ and seal____ this _____ Day of _____ A.D., 19____

_____ (Seal)

_____ (Seal)

PRACTICAL

1FD IN U.S.A. FORM 595 A   FRANK R. WALKER CO., PUBLISHERS, CHICAGO

How will these changes be provided for, and how will you be billed for the extra work?

It is frequently provided that the contractor may require payment in advance for work undertaken by change order.

Site Preparation

This is frequently the responsibility of the homeowner and refers to things like tree removal. The contractor will generally ask for a sentence that relieves him from sticking to the specified completion date if the homeowner has not fully prepared the site.

Building Permit

For almost any type of remodeling, you'll need a building permit. The contract should state that the contractor is responsible for this; whoever gets the permit is legally liable if the local inspector finds building code violations in the area under construction.

Other requirements, such as those that might be required by a home-owners association or an architectural review board, are the responsibility of the homeowner.

Dispute Settlement

Contracts also spell out what happens if something goes wrong. The fault can be either party—failure to pay or to provide access on the part of the homeowner, failure to complete the work as agreed on the part of the contractor.

If you specify that disputes will be settled by arbitration, specify who the arbitration panel will be. To locate possible arbitration groups, contact the American Arbitration Association (212-484-4000), the National Academy of Conciliators (214-638-5633), your state attorney general's office, or your local Better Business Bureau.

Breach of Contract

Everyone wants an out. Practices vary in different parts of the country, but the following provisions work for both homeowner and contractor.

After thirty days of nonpayment the contractor can submit notice to the homeowner; the homeowner has seven days to make full payment or the contractor is free to quit. The homeowner would be liable for payment for the work executed as well as for proven loss of time and materials for the contractor.

A homeowner who is dissatisfied with a contractor can give seven days written notice. If the situation is not rectified, then the homeowner can make arrangements to finish the job by whatever means are reasonable. The homeowner may deduct these costs from the amount due the contractor.

Advertising

Contractors generally like a sign outside the home stating who is doing the work. In addition, contractors may specify that pictures taken in progress and afterwards become his property and available for promotional use. (Some municipalities won't permit the display of signs, so check regulations before agreeing to signage.)

Safety

The contractor is responsible for maintaining safety and shall comply with all applicable rules and will indemnify the owner for all property loss or damage to the owner.

Hazardous Materials

Some contracts today spell out what will be done if hazardous materials (asbestos, radon, lead paint) are found on the job, specifying who is responsible for their removal, and any costs involved.

Financing Contingency

If you've come this far and still don't have the money for the project, then you should specify that the contract is void if you fail to obtain funds at a rate you can afford. (Some contracting companies offer financing, so if your job will be done by someone other than a sole proprietor you might ask if they have provisions for making loans.)

However, you should also know that contractors look for clients that are solvent. If the contractor senses that the money is not yet available for the work, most will find other jobs to fill their time until you're ready to write a check.

Finance Charge
Late payment is generally subject to a finance charge of $1^{1}/2\%$ a month on the unpaid balance until paid in full.

Rates for Additional Labor
If the homeowner has additional work to be performed during the course of the project, what rates will that work be charged at? Labor and carpentry are usually stipulated at an hourly rate. Materials and subcontract work is generally on a cost-plus basis.

Insurance
It is the responsibility of the contractor to obtain insurance that will cover personal injury, property damage, and worker's compensation. Copies of those coverages should be attached. (If you are not satisfied with the coverage you have, you can purchase umbrella insurance for very little to fill in any potential gaps in yours or the contractor's insurance.)

Notice of Your Right to Cancel
The Federal Trade Commission requires that the homeowner have three days in which to change his mind on any contract (for more than $25) if it was signed in an "impromptu" location, such as a home. To do so, you must mail your notice to the contractor within those three days or else deliver it or have it delivered to him within that time. For emergency repairs this provision is waived. (An example of a Notice of Cancellation can be found on page 95.)

The Non-Assignment Clause
It should be stated that the contractor will not give the project to someone else unless you both agree. And if the house is sold during construction, the contractor does not need to complete the job under the new owner.

These are the paragraphs that are covered in most contracts. Some of the other provisions that appear frequently follow.

Cleanup
Specify how this will be handled. If the debris is being tarped on your property, put in writing that the contractor is responsible for ultimate

NOTICE OF CANCELLATION

Date:_____

YOU MAY CANCEL THIS TRANSACTION, WITHOUT PENALTY OR OBLIGATION, WITHIN THREE BUSINESS DAYS FROM THE ABOVE DATE.

IF YOU CANCEL, ANY PROPERTY TRADED IN, ANY PAYMENTS MADE BY YOU UNDER THIS CONTRACT OF SALE, AND ANY NEGOTIABLE INSTRUMENT EXECU-TED BY YOU WILL BE RETURNED WITHIN TEN BUSINESS DAYS FOLLOWING RECEIPT BY THE SELLER OF YOUR CANCELLATION NOTICE, AND ANY SECUR-ITY INTEREST ARISING OUT OF THE TRANSACTION WILL BE CANCELLED.

IF YOU CANCEL, YOU MUST MAKE AVAILABLE TO THE SELLER AT YOUR RESIDENCE, IN SUBSTANTIALLY AS GOOD CONDITION AS WHEN RECEIVED, ANY GOODS DELIVERED TO YOU UNDER THIS CONTRACT OF SALE; OR YOU MAY, IF YOU WISH, COMPLY WITH THE INSTRUCTIONS OF THE SELLER REGARDING THE RETURN SHIPMENT OF THE GOODS AT THE SELLER'S EXPENSE AND RISK.

IF YOU DO MAKE THE GOODS AVAILABLE TO THE SELLER AND THE SELLER DOES NOT PICK THEM UP WITHIN TWENTY DAYS OF THE DATE OF YOUR NOTICE OF CANCELLATION, YOU MAY RETAIN OR DISPOSE OF THE GOODS AVAILABLE TO THE SELLER, OR IF YOU AGREE TO RETURN THE GOODS TO THE SELLER AND FAIL TO DO SO, THEN YOU REMAIN LIABLE FOR PERFOR-MANCE OF ALL OBLIGATIONS UNDER THE CONTRACT.

TO CANCEL THIS TRANSACTION, MAIL OR DELIVER A SIGNED AND DATED COPY OF THIS CANCELLATION NOTICE OR ANY OTHER WRITTEN NOTICE, OR SEND A TELEGRAM TO:
                    BRENNER BUILDERS, INC.
                    261 Washington Avenue
                    New Rochelle, New York 10801

NOT LATER THAN MIDNIGHT OF:_____

I HEREBY CANCEL THIS TRANSACTION. Date:_____

_____   _____
   (Buyer's Signature)   (Buyer's Signature)

I (We) hereby acknowledge receipt of TWO COPIES of this Notice of Cancellation Form, filled in with the name of the Contractor, its address, and the date by which I must cancel.

_____   _____
   (Buyer's Signature)   (Date of Receipt)

_____
   (Buyer's Signature)

removal of debris and state the condition you expect the property to be left in when the job is complete. "Broom clean" is generally the description for work done on the interior. If yours is exterior work, a contractor will generally state that he will return the yard to "rough-grade" finish, topsoil and landscape by other."

Special Instructions

Does this job involve any special circumstances? Is part of the house off limits? Do you want materials stored in a certain place? Are the old appliances supposed to be moved somewhere (basement? in-laws?). Put details in writing.

Completion Bonus

A completion bonus may make sense, particularly if you've been dislocated during the renovation. Suppose the homeowner is paying $3,000 per month in rent to live elsewhere during the work. The clause might specify that two thirds of that savings ($2,000) would go to the contractor as a completion bonus if he gets the family back in the house a month earlier than specified.

Penalty Clause

Penalty clauses, which fine the contractor for being late, are talked of more than actually used. If used, there would generally be a one-week grace period since home remodeling is never an exact science. Then the contract might specify that the contractor must pay the homeowner $100 for each week until substantial completion. To some extent, the penalty clause can end up penalizing both parties. If the contractor begins to lose too much money he may walk away from the job because he's lost his profit anyway. If you want to provide incentive, go for the positive. Establish a completion bonus instead.

For the Major Remodeling Job

If your remodeling job involves major work (a large addition or interior remodeling that involves several rooms) and is scheduled to take several months, it is particularly important that you work carefully through what your contract provides. This is particularly important because, as the homeowner, you are the more likely party to come up on the short end. If there's a midjob dispute, the contractor might walk. You're the one left without a roof and the inside of your walls exposed.

If you have any concern, have a lawyer review the contract. A large remodeling job is a major investment, and so you needn't rush into it. Take time to understand each stage of the project and see that it's all spelled out. Having a legal review will simply clarify any overlooked questions and help you feel that you've made the right decision.

INSIDER'S TIP

Cost-Plus Jobs

Both sides need to proceed carefully with the cost-plus job. It can be a perfectly legitimate way of operating, but additional details need to be spelled out. Contact the AIA for their time-and-materials contract.

- Exactly what is to be completed? This needs to be described carefully. All the contractor needs to hear to ruin the job is, "Hey, I'm not paying for you people to do that; that wasn't part of the job." Contemplate how you'll handle the unexpected. If the workers discover a rotten beam at 10 A.M., the contractor won't want them to sit around for a couple of hours while he tries to reach you to see if you'll pay for the beam to be replaced.
- Specify the hourly or daily rate of the workers; specify the sums that will be paid to subs.
- Spell out whether or not there will be a markup on materials.

Trusting your contractor is the most important thing in making a time-and-materials contract work out. If the two of you work well together and agree on specific checkpoints it can be a fine way to do business.

Additional Details

Ask the contractor to have her insurance company send you a certificate of insurance with you listed as the certificate holder as proof that she is adequately covered in case of property damage, personal injury claims, or accidents involving workers. You should be named as the insured under the workman's compensation coverage as well.

Discuss allowances and provide for them in the contract documents. A contractor may agree to provide door hardware or lighting, but you may want to provide input. Generally the contractor tells the homeowner the amount per fixture or the amount per doorknob that she has allowed for in the contract. Like decorators, contractors generally get a break on prices of fixtures and finish items, but in turn she charges a slight markup when selling it to you. When $50 is specified as the allowance for each doorknob, be sure to clarify whether that is the ultimate price to you or whether it's the contractor price on which there will be an additional markup. Should the homeowner choose something more expensive at a later time, the contractor will have to add an additional amount to cover the difference.

CONTRACTOR TIP

Keep the Job Intact

As details of the contract are worked out and the price is set, particularly on a big job . . . the homeowner or his architect sometimes decides to take control of some aspect of the project himself to save money. I've had the air-conditioning work, the cabinetry and the supplying of plumbing fixtures removed from a contract after initially pricing the job with those elements included. Fine. We proceed.

On a major home renovation, the homeowner withdrew the new boiler and radiators from my part of the contract because he "knew someone who could do it cheaper." Fine. What no one considered was that my price included the carpentry to reframe around the radiators—the plumber's price didn't. But the misfortune continued. The radiators leaked and damaged some of the new flooring we installed. The homeowner had to pay us to replace what was damaged. Had it been in my part of the contract, I would have been legally obligated to replace the damaged sections at no additional expense to the owner.

What started out as a way to save money ended up costing the homeowner more—more for me to frame the radiators, which had to be billed out separately, and more for me to replace what was damaged.

Throughout the book, we talk about the importance of handling things "in phase." If I can do what needs to be done at the time it needs to be done, I can save you money. If I have to do it at a different time, it costs both of us more. If you've hired a general contractor, let him control the job. "In phase" will keep everyone happy.

What to Do with the Official Documents

Once everything has been agreed to, all parties will sign three copies of the contract and initial three sets of the plans. (One for the homeowner; one for the contractor; and one for the designer or architect.) Your original copy of the contract and the initialed set of plans should be put in a safe deposit box for safekeeping.

Ask to be provided with an extra copy of the contract and a working set of the plans. They will be useful tools throughout the remodeling process.

CONTRACT WORKSHEET

Contractor _____ Homeowner _____

Company Name _____ Address _____

License No._____ Telephone _____

Address _____

Telephone _____

Architect or Designer _____

Address _____

Telephone _____

Start date: _____ Estimated completion date:_____

Overall scope of the project _____

_____

List of specific work to be done _____

_____

_____

Describe any contractor-provided materials that must be a certain brand (e.g., make of refrigerator) or quality (e.g., type of wood for deck) _____

_____

_____

List any homeowner-provided items _____

_____

List any work the homeowner is responsible for outside the contract

_____

_____

Site preparation responsibilities _____

Day-to-day clean-up expectations _____

_____

End-of job clean-up responsibilities _____

_____

Price: _____

Payment schedule:

Completed task   Amount to be paid

_____   _____

_____   _____

Rates for additional labor _____

Penalty/bonus provisions _____

After filling in this worksheet, review the chapter again for some of the additional provisions and stipulations your contract should cover in order to create a fair agreement for all parties.

When Your Contractor Fails You

Unfortunately, home remodeling is risky business; there are a lot of fly-by-night operations and the Better Business Bureau files overflow with complaints.

Throughout this book, we make every effort to see that you were working with reputable people. We've stressed the importance of checking the contractor's license, calling several references, visiting a work site, and putting together a careful contract, among many other recommendations. We've also warned about paying too much money in advance. If your payments were well matched to the completion checkpoints, then with luck you have not paid out too much money.

But what happens if something goes wrong? Here are some suggestions:

- If you followed the suggestions in chapter 7, your contract should have provided an arbitration clause. Invoke it. If you agreed to binding arbitration, then both sides will be able to present their case and go on from there.
- There should also be a provision for "breach of contract." You may lose a little in the deal, but with luck you can pull out of your contract and hire someone else to finish the job.
- If he really did skip town, your only recourse is to contact an attorney who can begin to review the situation with you and offer professional advice. Be sure to notify the Better Business Bureau and your state licensing agency so that other consumers will be forewarned.

Homeowner Checklist

- If your contractor or designer does not have a standard contract to use as a boilerplate, contact the American Institute of Architects, the American Homeowners Foundation, or hire an attorney to draft one for you.
- Create a contract that is fair to both parties.
- Be as detailed as possible in your contract.
- Tie the payment schedule to specific stages of completion. Your payments should bear a reasonable relationship to the amount of work performed or the expenses incurred at each stage.
- Consider having a lawyer review the contract for you.
- Put your signed contract and spec sheet in a safe deposit box; ask for another set to use as a working document.

Chapter 8

Battening down the Hatches: Preparing for Construction

Now your project is getting exciting. The contract is signed, and soon a crew will arrive to make your dream a reality. If your anxiety level has heightened that's normal. At about this stage, most homeowners acquire a how-will-we-live-through-this-and-pay-for-it? feeling. Fortunately, there are positive ways to use this nervous energy.

Get Final Permission to Remodel

Although you, your architect or designer, and the contractor may all have been in touch with your local building department, it's time to make your project official by filing for a building permit. This document authorizes you to begin your remodeling project and is issued only after a local inspector has examined your final plans, confirming that your project conforms with all local and state building codes, requirements, and zoning laws. If you needed a variance and have received it, the inspector will be certain that variance and plans agree.

After any structural change to your home—including the addition of a deck or pool—local building departments must inspect the job to verify that the work performed complies with local building codes. Only after a final inspection (which is usually the last of several performed at specific times during the construction), will you be granted a certificate of occupancy (C.O.). This form, issued by the local government, describes your home exactly and legalizes your right to occupy it. If you ever decide to sell your home, you will be unable to do so without a valid C.O. Some communities also levy fines if you have delayed in getting a new C.O. What's more, if it isn't up to date, you can also run into trouble with your home insurance coverage. Companies may refuse to pay out on a claim and may even cancel the policy if you don't have a legitimate C.O.

Generally, your contractor will be the one to file for the permit. Make sure that he does. Building permits are required for almost everything:

structural changes, additions, expansions, enclosures, room conversions, site changes, excavations, and mechanical work. Only home repair is exempt from the permit requirement.

At the time he files for the permit, your contractor will have to show that he has the necessary insurance to do the job (general liability, workers' compensation, disability coverage).

Local ordinances like this were created to protect you. What you'll gain from it is assurance that the person you've hired is properly insured. You'll be guaranteed regular inspections (the foundation, framing, wiring, plumbing, and insulation will all be checked), and you will be safeguarded from shoddy workmanship at each of these stages.

Business Details

Determine the amounts of insurance coverage your contractor is carrying. Inquire about liability coverage and worker's compensation (in case property is damaged or someone is hurt on premises during the course of the job) for you and the contractor. (Have you received your certificate of insurance from the contractor? If not, be sure to get it before work begins.)

Let your own insurance agent know that work is going to start soon and ask whether you should increase coverage now. Some homeowners' insurance companies require you to notify the agent within 90 days of starting any work that increases the property value by $5,000 or more. This is to keep in effect the guaranteed-replacement-cost coverage. If your financing is coming in the form of a bulk payment, you'd be well advised to set up a special account for it. This will help you keep track of expenses for tax purposes, and it will keep the money safely earmarked for its intended purpose. If you get a money market account with check-writing privileges, you can earn interest on the balance while still having money available to make payments at the appropriate times. Also inquire if there is any supplementary insurance you need to be covered against damage caused by fire and theft.

Set up a special file for your construction bills, change orders, and correspondence you may have concerning the job. It will provide ready reference while the job is going on and complete documentation for tax purposes later on.

If any of the workers, such as the cabinetmakers, are being hired by you instead of through the contractor, call them. They should come for an on-site inspection. Encourage them to double-check all measurements while they are there. One cabinetmaker discovered that in drawing the plans an architect had inflated a family's kitchen by nine inches. If the cabinetmaker hadn't run a check, there would have been many problems when it came time for installation. It never hurts to double-check everything.

Start Making Decisions

"Decision-fatigue" hits many homeowners as the job continues, so resolve what you can in advance.

Develop a list of all the items that need to be selected for the job. Although you have likely selected major cabinetry, ask your contractor (and architect or designer), what else could be decided ahead of time. If it's a "contractor-provided" item to be selected by the homeowner, ask what the dollar allowance is for that item since it will be a contractor expense. (You can spend more, but you'll pay the difference.)

CONTRACTOR TIP

The Value of Planning

Thinking ahead will save you time and money. To illustrate this, I can tell you of a job where one "little" change caused a major delay. We were remodeling a bathroom when the homeowner informed me that she had changed her mind about the tile; she had ordered something different and it would arrive in six weeks. (We would have been ready to install her original choice in two weeks.) She also mentioned she had found a less expensive tile-layer and was going to use him for that part of the job. My crew worked for another ten days and then had to halt work on that job, because no work could proceed until the tile was installed.

The new tile finally came in and her tile-layer put it up crooked. She had us come back to remove it, then we waited another couple of months while more tile was ordered.

This one "little" change cost us (contractor and homeowner) five additional months. Instead of being finished in June as anticipated, we finally finished in late November. From a contractor's standpoint it was difficult, but I can tell you the family suffered too. There was no sense in putting the house back together until we were finished. What's more, a husband, wife, and two teens shared one bath for five more months than would have been necessary had she stayed with her original tile choice.

If your plans are detailed, you may have already selected many of these items. If not, now is the time to do it.

- Lighting and lighting fixtures. (If you're thinking of trying something new, ask the contractor, electrician, or architect to find homes where you can see it in place.)
- Bathroom fixtures: type and color of sink, shower body, tub, toilet, etc.
- Kitchen appliances and details such as exact faucet, type of spray hose, and sink style.
- Drawer pulls and cabinet knobs (for kitchen, bath, or built-ins in any room).
- Tile color and type.
- Stone or marble for masonry project.
- Type or color of hardwood flooring.
- Brick or wood siding.
- Window styles and type. Thermal? Single- or double-pane?
- Paint colors. (Even if the contractor isn't responsible for painting, you'll want to be ready for a separate painting crew as soon as the contractor is finished.)
- Trim (moldings). Do you want something new or something to match the existing trim? (Your contractor should have books or samples to show you.)
- Door hardware.
- Specialty items: fireplace, mantel, built-in safe, sound or phone system, or a household intercom.

Protecting Your Yard

With many remodeling jobs, yard preparation is an important aspect of getting ready. If you're putting on an addition major equipment will be on site, and, even for a project where the remodeling is entirely internal, dumpsters must sometimes be placed on your property rather than in the street. You'll want to discuss with the contractor how your yard will be affected and take appropriate steps.

- If trees need to be removed, get estimates and schedule removal.
- If you have shrubbery that you would like to preserve, contact a landscaper and get some opinions on which plants might be temporarily relocated and saved.
- If a tree needn't be taken down but might be in the way, talk to the contractor. Ask if they can erect a four-foot high temporary fence at the drip line of the tree to keep the equipment off the root system. (The "drip line" is the furthest point at which water

Yard Prep, Practically Speaking

Long before we signed a contract for our addition, I talked to tree specialists about the removal of a 100-foot oak tree, and I brought in a landscaper who talked to me about what he could do to save the plantings. Before we began construction in October, the landscaper uprooted many bushes and wrapped the root balls in burlap. He gave me explicit instructions to water the bagged shrubs if the weather was dry, but three kids, men all over the place, and a giant mud hole between the bushes and me meant that I got a hose out to

them exactly once. Despite this neglect, everything survived to be replanted the next spring.

We also had one large red maple that I asked the workers to protect with a temporary fence. The fence went down under the bulldozer a couple of times, but the tree has now seen its third spring since construction.

By planning ahead, we were able to save many beautiful, older plants we would have otherwise lost. We also saved money because it was less expensive to preserve the plants than replace them.

drip froms the tree leaves. It gives a good indication of the size of the root system that needs to be protected.)

To Stay or Not to Stay? That May Be the Question

If your home is going to be totally torn up, you'd be wise to move out. If you have any question about livableness, consult your contractor.

Work generally goes more quickly in an unoccupied space, so if you have any alternatives there are advantages. Some people plan to be on vacation during demolition, others rent a home, others occupy rooms above garages. If you have to be out of the house, consider offering economic incentives for the contractor to stay on schedule. Any provision such as this should go into the contract (see chapter 7).

Supervision is still important. Stop by frequently and let the contractor know that you can meet him at almost any time if there is a particularly important part of the work going on.

Items to Discuss with the Contractor

Schedule a meeting to discuss final preparation details that need to be taken care of before construction begins. (Some of this should have been put in writing, as discussed in chapter 7.) Here are some of the items you will want to review.

Items to be saved and reused. Walk through your home, and identify any items in the area that will be under construction that are to be saved (doors, windows, chandelier, etc.). Ask what arrangements will be made to safeguard these items.

Priorities. Do you need the work done in a particular order, and does it make sense to the contractor? One homeowner wanted to get back into his home office as soon as possible, so the contractor established a schedule that permitted that work to be completed first.

Telephone. Is the contractor having a line installed or using a cellular phone? If the workers will be using your telephone, remind the contractor of what contractual agreement you reached regarding the phone bill (see chapter 7).

Worker space. The workers will need a staging area, often the basement, garage, or some part of the new construction. Discuss with your contractor the best place for them to set up base and also determine a specific door for their entrance and exit. It will make life easier in the long run.

Bathroom facilities. If a portable toilet is to be provided by the contractor, confirm that arrangements have been made. If not, discuss which bathroom they'll have access to.

Separation of space. You will want some privacy during the job. If you're putting on an addition that is separate from the main part of the house, you may want to consider ways they can divide the house. Can a plywood wall be erected between the family living quarters and the section under construction? A padlocked door in the temporary wall could permit access between the two areas. If walling off the family living space isn't possible, point out rooms that you consider "off limits" until they notify you that the work (such as installation of air-conditioning ducts) cannot continue until they disrupt those rooms as well.

Home access. How will the contractor come and go? One homeowner requested that the contractor use a basement door with a different lock from the rest of the house and provided him with that key only. That permits the family to lock up at other times knowing that no one else can gain access to their home. Other families ask their alarm company to assign the contractor a temporary code. That way the house can be fully alarmed at all times, and after the work is done the code can be changed. For large jobs, homeowners have had their alarm companies rework the system temporarily so that the part of the house occupied by the family was fully alarmed while the part under construction was separate and not alarmed during the early stages.

Car access. If your driveway is large enough, you may be able to share it with workers. Discuss where you'd like to park, and request that they not block you in with their trucks.

Health safeguards. Do you have special requests regarding safeguarding the family's health? Discuss them at this time. What steps will the contractor take to minimize the dust? Should the family vacate for a certain period to reduce exposure to the dust?

Home protection. Plastic tarps should be draped over furniture that is not being used by the family but is still near the area where the work is being done. Plastic of at least 4-mil thickness should be taped over all openings into the living quarters. Apply it to the inside of the door jamb or trim and saddle of the door using duct tape so that when the tape is removed, you only have to repaint the trim, not the whole wall (see sketch on page 00). If the work will create a lot of dusty traffic past closets, either relocate the contents of the closets or ask that the contractor put plastic over the closet doors to help lessen the amount of dust that will get in. For closets that will be used regularly, set aside a supply of old towels. By stuffing a towel along the bottom of the door each morning before the workers arrive, you can greatly reduce the dirt and grit that will get into the closet.

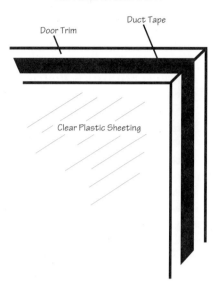

THE PROPER WAY TO
COVER A DOORWAY

Door Trim

Duct Tape

Clear Plastic Sheeting

duct tape on trim, not on walls

- Floor coverings (drop cloths or special paper provided by the contractor) should be placed over all floors that will encounter workers. If the family reclaims these areas at night, you may want the drop cloths picked up each evening so that family members or guests don't trip over them. Coverings should be changed or washed when they get dirty.
- Heating and air-conditioning ducts in the room(s) under construction should be taped with plastic so that dust doesn't circulate through them into the rest of the house.

- Discuss which walls and floors you intend to refinish or repaint and ask that workers take special care with the other areas that aren't going to be redone. You can't expect miracles, especially in tight halls and doorways, but do have the contractor remind them that one piece of duct tape attached carelessly can result in an unnecessary redo or patch job.
- Remember that an attempt should be made to protect anything you care about. Homeowners who had a driveway made of hand-laid decorative brick requested that a plywood and tarp frame be made to protect it. Preventative steps cost extra, but the money spent will be far less than what it would cost to replace a treasured item.

Cleanup expectations. If a full and complete cleanup is expected daily, it will reduce the amount of work the crew can accomplish simply because work time will have to be spent cleaning up. However, they should do a cursory cleanup daily. Have a two-way discussion about what you can tolerate and what you simply can't. (Even at best, the area—and possibly your living quarters, if you're not walled off—is still going to be much dustier than usual.)

Debris management. Will a dumpster be used for construction trash? If so, where will it be placed? If not, what method will the contractor employ?

Responsibility. Remind the contractor that you will work together on issues of safety and security but that ultimately, you are entrusting him or her with maintaining the safety of your home and possessions.

HOMEOWNER TIP

Document, Document!

Although most of your discussions may have taken place around your kitchen table, you're entering into a major business deal and it should be treated as such.

The best protection you can give yourself is to make notes after homeowner-contractor discussions. (Use your notebook.) Write down the date of the conversation and what was decided. Comments concerning your discussion of the thirteen items listed earlier could be your first page. Then when someone says, "What did we decide about. . . ?" you'll have it all right there.

No matter how "simple" your job, you'll find that an extraordinary number of details are involved.

CONTRACTOR TIP

Don't Expect Miracles

Remodeling is messy, dirty work, and despite careful efforts to protect your home damage is going to occur. Heavy machinery may be involved, and few blades of grass can withstand this kind of traffic.

If you've just redone your floors hold off awhile on remodeling. We won't be able to leave them "as good as new." We'll do everything we can to take good care of your property and possessions, but just be aware that our equipment is heavy and we're only human.

A little realism will go a long way when it comes to the schedule. Although we have every intention of meeting our deadline, things happen. Bad weather will delay outdoor work, carpenters get the flu, and materials sometimes arrive late. We're putting our best foot forward, but we'll appreciate some leeway too.

Furniture: Whose Responsibility Is It?

Contractors want furniture moved out of all affected construction areas, and this can mean a lot of moving. Ask your contractor what he suggests about the furniture for your particular job.

Discuss with the contractor where you plan to store furniture. Treasured pieces of furniture should either be stored off premises or put in a part of the house where the workers won't need to be. Your family's basement might be a possibility, or call a personal warehouse in your area to see what it would cost to rent space. (For a 10' × 10' warehouse that can hold up to four rooms of furniture fees vary from about $250

CONTRACTOR TIP

The Happy Contractor

If the bathroom is to be gutted and updated, a happy contractor is one whose client family has removed everything in his path—from the front foyer, up the stairs, down the hall, and into the bedroom and bath. Although on the surface this demand seems silly, it is impossible for workers to guarantee that they will be able to get an item like a cast-iron bathtub out of the house without scraping it against something.

Making Way for the Workers

Packing things away and finding storage space is not fun, but the more you can put away during the renovation, the better it will be. During my renovation, I packed away dishes, art, lamps, and small items. But I should have done more. We couldn't use the living room or dining room anyway, and I should have stored that furniture and the area rugs off premises. Out of necessity, the workers moved furniture from one part of the house to another when it got in their way, but it certainly wasn't a kid-glove treatment. They didn't like having to do the furniture shifting, and it made me anxious to watch them.

Another homeowner whose family living space was being reduced to two bedrooms and a bath dedicated her living room to a storage area. "We set up aisles of bureaus and boxes, and I created a map of what I'd stored where. When anyone needed something beyond the obvious, I pulled out my map and could tell them, 'Aisle 3, Box 4.'"

---

per month in a metropolitan area to $100 or less elsewhere in the country. The less space you need, the less it will cost you. Some warehouses will provide a truck for the move.)

How will you get everything rearranged? Friends, relatives, or neighbors might be willing to help you move furniture. If not, call a moving company to see if one or two movers might work for you for a couple of hours. The contractor may also be able to spare someone to work for you freelance.

If you're remodeling during the winter and it's going to be cold, loan out your plants for awhile. The household temperature will be erratic, and many homeowners have seen their hothouse plants suffer an early frost.

Homeowner Preparations

Clear the rooms. For major remodeling projects or any work that involves the dining room or kitchen, pack up all fine china, dinnerware, art, and novelty items. (More details on preparing for kitchen remodeling below.) You may want to do the packing yourself, or call a moving company who can send someone over with appropriate boxes and get everything packed for you in a few hours time.

Put valuables in storage. Even the best contractors will tell you that, although they know most of the workers on the job, it is impossible to vouch for the honesty of a new employee or one of the subcontractors. You can help safeguard your possessions by placing as many valuables as possible in your safe deposit box. A friend or relative might be willing to store your silver, coin collections, or a particularly valuable camera. Cash and valuables that must remain at home should be well hidden. You may also want to move computers and their disks and keepsakes and photo albums to protect them from damage caused by dust.

Protect files and bookcases. Tape sheets over file cabinets, bookcases, and closets to reduce the amount of dust that seeps through cracks.

Preservation of personal tools. As a homeowner, the best thing to do is to tuck away all tools, extension cords, and brooms before construction starts. Place them together in the garage or basement and cover with a drop cloth. The contractor expects to provide these things, and you should make it absolutely necessary that he does.

CONTRACTOR TIP

So What Happens to the Tools?

Workers don't intend to walk off with the homeowner's tools, but imagine this situation: Joe, the carpenter, needs a screwdriver to remove an outlet from a wall that is to be demolished. After setting up, he finds that he has left his screwdriver in the truck. Wearing a T-shirt and remembering that it's 35 degrees and raining outside, Joe recalls that Harry Homeowner has a brand new tool box only a few steps away on the basement workbench. Does Joe really want to climb over the table saw, run upstairs and outdoors into the freezing rain in his T-shirt? Of course not. So Joe "borrows" Harry Homeowner's screwdriver. He uses it for one minute and places it in his tool belt. At the end of the day, Joe is packing up his tools and notices Harry's screwdriver. He places it in his truck in a special spot so he will remember to return it tomorrow. But tomorrow is Saturday and Joe's day off. Joe's son, Joe Junior, needs a screwdriver to fix his bicycle. He remembers seeing one last night on the floor of his Dad's truck. . . .

Joe made the decision most of us would have made, but, of course, the story should have ended with the return of the screwdriver to its rightful owner. Pack up your tools, and you won't have to worry.

If the Construction Involves the Kitchen

The majority of today's remodeling projects involve kitchens, so at some point most readers will find themselves literally wondering where their next meal will come from. Even when things go well, the family is likely to be without a kitchen for six to eight weeks. Here are some recommendations to help you get through it.

- If your remodeling project only involves the kitchen, don't let the work crew touch the existing one until the new cabinets (and any other specialty item that might stop progress) are in your possession. Many times a crew will start the demolition work and then be forced to halt because the kitchen cabinets have not yet arrived. (If you're doing other parts of the house, this is less significant as they can work elsewhere if there is a cabinet delay.)
- When the cabinets do arrive, inspect them with the contractor. Cabinets that are damaged in shipping will need to be sent back. (After co-inspecting the cabinets, both you and the contractor should sign a paper testifying that the cabinets are in good condition. Should the workmen accidentally damage something during installation, you'll have proof that the cabinets were undamaged upon arrival.) Inspected cabinets should be covered (for protection) and stored in your basement or garage. Only then should the work proceed.
- Ask the contractor where you might put a temporary kitchen. Contractors have seen a lot of temporary setups, and most will have suggestions based on your household requirements. The space chosen should give you access to water for cooking and washing dishes, a place for food preparation, and room for a table and chairs. Usually a basement or bedroom near a bath fit the above criteria. Once you have chosen the location of this temporary kitchen, you will need the following items:

  - microwave oven
  - refrigerator (does not have to be in the same room)
  - portable or gas burner
  - basic pots and pans
  - paper plates, cups, towels, and napkins (yes, it is environmentally wasteful, but perhaps you can make up for it later in some other way)
  - minimal dishes and silverware (if the above offends you)
  - sponge, dishwashing liquid, towels
  - boxes or temporary cupboard or closet for food storage

- table and chairs for the family
- patience

Family Considerations

How will the disruption of the household affect the children? This depends on how long the renovation is expected to last and how altered the children's lives will be. Adding a powder room off the living room probably won't affect them much, but remodeling a kitchen or anything that moves them out of their bedrooms will be unsettling. Here are some suggestions:

- Include them early in the process so that it will feel like a family project. Let your children see plans. Talk about why you're doing it and what you'll be adding that they will like, for instance, a big family room, new bedroom, porch, etc.
- Present the experience as an adventure. In the beginning, most kids think that relying on the local pizza parlor and McDonald's for dinner is going to be grand. (They forget that even french fries don't taste very good when Mom is grumpy.) And if children must bunk together temporarily, describe it as the ultimate sleep-over party.
- If a child must vacate his room, remind him of the wonders of the new house you're creating. For children preschool age and younger, pack away their less-used toys and make room for their favorites in a sibling's room. School-age children will probably want to help in the selection and temporary placement of their belongings.
- Children ages two to seven might enjoy having their own child-sized tool belt so they feel a part of the action.
- After workers have left for the day, let your children give tours (supervised by you) to relatives and, if the space is safe, to their friends.
- Give an estimated finish time. "By Christmas we'll have a new family room where you can play your video games."
- Discuss rules. There will most likely be periods when the house is unsafe. Stress the importance of obeying new rules such as not climbing on the piles of lumber stacked in the yard or not playing outside when the roofer is working. Workers should be presented as authority figures in charge of your children's safety, and your children should know to take any warnings from them seriously.
- Help the workers and the children become acquainted. There may be a carpenter who actually enjoys your son following him

around, but there may also be an electrician who dislikes children and acts that way. Remember, too, the contractor's job would be easier if he didn't have to work around on-site kids. To avoid having your children yelled at by the workers—or actually hurt—keep an eye out at all times.

- Tell your pediatrician that you are undertaking a construction project. She can help you evaluate the risks to your family.

The Happy Pet Is a Safe Pet

To make the proper provisions for your pets, the family will need to weigh both the extent of the construction project and the type of pet.

Birds
Birds react poorly to the temperature changes caused by workers coming in and out, as well as the increased level of dust in the air. And paint fumes can actually lead to Tweety's untimely demise so it's a wise idea to get them off the premises while the work is being done.

Cats
Cats generally hide throughout the experience, but be certain that you see your cat at least once a day. (Most usually check in at feeding time.) Should yours be missing at some point, you'll want to stop work until your pet is found. A cat who crawls into a wall space thinking it's a safe retreat may wind up being inadvertently trapped by the workers.

Dogs
A calm dog who is used to sleeping in a pet crate may adapt to spending some daytime hours in the crate as well. Or there may be a room where the dog can stay during the day with no risk of being hurt or being let out accidentally.

If the backyard will be the site of serious disruption and your dog is used to spending time in the yard, specify that your contractor should be responsible for putting up and taking down a temporary fence so that there will be a safe area for your dog during the major construction phase. Obviously, no tools, debris, or equipment should be placed in this area, and the contractor should be responsible for a thorough cleanup of the rest of the backyard before the renovation is finished.

Consult your vet. The construction is going to be noisy, and may be upsetting to a nervous or high-strung animal. A pet who can't be kept away from the action is in danger of getting hurt or escaping from the premises. There may be periods during the work when you will need to board the animal or ask a neighbor to take him for the day.

Final Details

Contact the alarm company. Tell the company you're about to undertake a construction project. Dust can damage or set off motion detectors and other electronic equipment. You will want to learn from them what they can do to keep the alarm operable while protecting it from potential damage. If the contractor will need to be able to operate the alarm (if you set it and workers are still coming and going), ask that the company assign a separate code for contractor use during this limited period of time. And if you want to rewire part of the system to bypass the part of the house that's under construction, ask that it be done now.

This is also a good time to discuss with an alarm expert any additional questions you have about relocating the alarm system or keypads. Although an architect or designer may have specified certain details concerning alarm placement, the alarm people may have their own opinions. Try to give the company an approximate date for returning to rewire the system while the walls are still open.

Call or visit the neighbors. In most neighborhoods, construction work is disruptive. Your normally quiet street may now have workmen's cars and trucks filling up the area. For "good neighbor" relations, it's well worth letting them know a few things:

- what you're doing
- when you're starting
- how long you expect it to take
- who they should contact if the work disturbs them (usually the contractor or job foreman)

Any remodeling you do will most likely benefit the neighborhood housing prices in the long run, but it's hard for Mrs. Smith to remember that if the workers' trucks are making it difficult for her bridge club to park nearby.

If you feel a neighbor will be significantly inconvenienced (or that the neighbor is likely to make life miserable for your crew), send a fruit basket or bottle of wine. You can add a note of apology for any inconvenience the work may cause.

If the contractor is wise, he'll make the rounds with you or after you. A little advance consideration may lead to future referrals, and it can directly affect the speed of the project. Should the crew need an especially early start on some roof work in order to beat a coming rainstorm, a neighbor who has met the contractor personally will probably drop by to complain personally rather than calling the police to report that a local ordinance on morning start-time is being violated.

Start a Household Scrapbook

Take your "before" pictures now. This can be the start of an interesting document of your home remodeling adventure. To come will be pictures of the dumpster, the backhoe, the crew carrying things over and around your property. If you have children, you'll be capturing them at a certain age when they lived through what will be a most memorable family experience.

Attitude

The single most important factor in surviving a home remodeling project is family attitude. If you've hired a contractor you like and have done your best to prepare the household, then try viewing it as an exciting adventure. The experience will be a test of your planning, foresight, patience, congeniality under stress, and your tolerance for dust, but the end result is going to be something you've saved for, planned for, and want very much.

It's exciting to have a whole group of people showing up every day to make your dream a reality. You might as well enjoy it!

Homeowner Checklist for Construction Preparation

- Make certain that your contractor has obtained the necessary building permit.
- Call your insurance agent to be certain you're adequately covered throughout the construction phase.
- Start a file for renovation-related receipts and documents.
- Make as many decisions in advance as possible.
- Call tree-removal services or landscapers, if necessary, and get estimates.
- Talk to the contractor about:
  - preservation of any items such as doors
  - priorities
  - telephone
  - bathroom facilities
  - separation of space between workers and family
  - household access
  - health safeguards
  - protection of floors and walls
  - cleanup
  - debris management
  - overall responsibility

- Decide on the disposition of your furniture and make arrangements.
- The homeowner should:
  - clear out rooms
  - store valuables
  - hide tools
- When remodeling a kitchen:
  - Don't let them start work until cabinets have arrived and been inspected.
  - Set up a temporary kitchen.
- Prepare family.
- Consider what to do with pets.
- Take care of final details:
  - Contact alarm company.
  - Notify neighbors.

Chapter 9

The Honeymoon Phase: Construction Begins

The "honeymoon phase" is the beginning of any new relationship, and like any other honeymoon the excitement of beginning will help you view these early days of remodeling through rose-colored glasses. Bask in this phase as long as you can because there's nothing easy about listening to the sound of workers taking a sledgehammer to your old bathroom tile or watching as they drive a backhoe through your side garden.

Regardless of whether the first step of your work is demolition or digging a foundation, the process can be overwhelming—and very, very dirty. Without a doubt, this will be the dustiest honeymoon you ever had.

Planning for Debris

A dumpster is the most common way of managing the debris, and its dramatic arrival (a huge truck huffs and puffs into your normally quiet neighborhood, and there's a lot of activity while the dumpster is properly placed) is often the first sign that your project is really going to get underway. These containers look like (and are) a truck bed and they come in two sizes: small, 8' × 12', (about the size of a compact car) for smaller remodeling jobs; and the "stretch" model, 8' × 22' (the size of a Winnebago) for major rehabs.

Sometimes the dumpster will be placed on the lawn, other times it will have to sit in your driveway and may block the driveway or garage.

Some communities prohibit dumpsters so debris is placed in a designated spot in the yard and covered with a tarp every night. (Tarping debris is also used if there is not a good location for a dumpster or if the job isn't large enough to warrant it.) You and your contractor should select a safe site. If you have a dog and the site you select is an area your pet has access to, ask the contractor to have the crew erect a temporary fence so that your dog won't be hurt climbing through the trash.

Discuss, too, how the rubbish will be tarped and emphasize that you want it well covered. An unexpected wind storm could turn your yard (and street) into a litter-strewn eyesore.

In either case, the contractor is generally responsible for cleanup of the area where the debris was or where the dumpster was placed. If reseeding the lawn becomes necessary, it usually is the homeowner's responsibility.

A Word about Dumpsters and Debris

Dumpsters and debris piles are hazardous because of the type of rubbish that goes into them. There may be broken glass, tile shards, and any number of dangerous things. Therefore, treat the situation seriously if you notice the neighborhood kids expressing interest in your dumpster or tarped trash. Remove from their mind the idea that it is acceptable to be near this trash.

Getting rid of debris is costly—extremely costly in densely settled parts of the country where land (and landfills) are at a premium. Remember that the dumpster belongs to the contractor, and one of the ways she figures costs is by estimating how many dumpster-loads of debris your job will be. Although most contractors have no objection to your putting a few things into the dumpster, ask first. She may not mind but might prefer that you wait until the second dumpster-load. And should you decide to clean out your entire basement or let your neighbor use your dumpster when he cleans out his, the contractor may have to charge you extra.

That said, you may also notice that not all of the debris that goes into your dumpster will be yours. When a toilet shows up in the dumpster for your kitchen demolition debris, you'll likely be puzzled. "Dumpster management" is at work. The contractor may be finishing another job where the dumpster is no longer needed or doing a small job that will not have a great deal of debris. He'll use the dumpster he has at your home for the one or two items that he has from the smaller job. Sometimes, too, the contractor will agree to do a favor for a trades-

---

INSIDER'S TIP

Using the Street as Your Driveway

If the dumpster or the placement of the debris blocks the use of your driveway, you will probably have to park on the street overnight. In some communities, this is prohibited without a permit. Check with your local police department to see if any special permits are required if a car must be left out overnight.

man. Maybe the reason you got the best plumber in town to agree to do your bathroom when he really didn't have time is because he and your contractor have an agreement over occasional use of dumpsters.

Proper dumpster management also lets your dumpster disappear sooner than it might if it were only holding debris from your renovation. When a contractor gets to the point that there isn't much debris on your job, he'll take it away. Any excess rubbish will now be taken to his next job and your front yard will look a little more normal.

Setting up Shop

In earlier meetings with the contractor, you've likely discussed where it will be most convenient for the workers to set up shop (garage, basement, etc.), and this will be where all tools, supplies, and tarps will be stored each night. Workers will probably arrive with a job box for safe storage of tools. Job boxes are large boxes, ranging from the size of a toy box to the size of a refrigerator, which can be padlocked closed each night. If you have small children, stress the importance of unplugging and putting away all power tools at the end of the day. Some families have gone so far as to request that workers unplug the tools whenever they aren't using them, but this will slow the job and it is your responsibility to keep children out of work areas during the day.

After hours is another story. You should impress on workers that they must secure the tools each night before they go home. Remember, too, that with or without power tools a worksite is no place for a child. There will be dangerous objects around, and something as small as a stray nail can easily puncture the sole of a shoe. Keep the kids away from the work area as much as possible.

HOMEOWNER TIP

Ask for Introductions

Though we'll stress throughout that your contact should be with the contractor, the carpenters, plumbers, electricians, and all the rest of the gang will be spending a lot of time in your house. Tell the contractor you'd like to be introduced, or at least ask him for the names of the people who will be working there. Home remodeling is an intense experience and having a friendly relationship with those who are helping rebuild your house will make it a more pleasant one.

House Preparation

Upon arrival, the first thing the workers will do is the house preparation. They'll arrive with tarps, plastic sheeting, and duct tape. As we discussed in the last chapter, a plywood wall should be built or a plastic sheet should be draped to create a dust- and privacy-buffer between the part of the house where you'll be living and the area where the construction will be underway. Even if there are doors that can be closed, ask them to drape plastic anyway. The amount of dust that will be stirred up will warrant maximum protection, and the plastic over a door can be hung so that you can lift and go under one side.

Discuss with the workers where the tarp will be hung. Because duct tape can pull off paint and destroy wallpaper, remind them which of the walls will be redone anyway. This will minimize the amount of cosmetic repair work that will be necessary when they leave.

Workers should also tape heating and air-conditioning ducts in the affected areas so that dust doesn't travel through the air conduit system.

Smoke alarms also need to be covered; dust sets them off in the same way that smoke does. Some contractors use smoke alarm covers that can be removed nightly. Others will tape plastic over a box for the duration of the job, which deactivates the alarm for that period of time. This isn't a good idea. A home undergoing remodeling really should have a working smoke alarm system in place. You have extra people working with

---

CONTRACTOR TIP

Guaranteeing a Slow Start

When I walk into a home with the kids' toys strewn across the hallway and the furniture still in place in the area where we'll be working, this costs us (and the homeowner) at least a half day.

If we're working in a family room, empty out the space, and the hallway leading to it. If we're renovating a kitchen, empty all the cupboards. We're happy to move the refrigerator, and if everything else is done before that the major

items will only take a few minutes. You'll save yourself grief by being prepared.

And if the job in the kitchen is a small one and leaves the kitchen intact, please give us the space for the eight or nine hours we've specified as our work day. Take the kids out for meals for a few days and pick up your coffee at Dunkin' Donuts. The clearer our access, the sooner we'll be out of your way.

Ordering Specialty Items

If you've assumed responsibility for ordering anything—from specialty tiles to custom cabinetry or light fixtures—check on the order or place it immediately. When the workers are ready for them, you need to have the items on site.

high voltage equipment in a house filled with dust particles and wood shavings.

If your fire alarm system is hard wired to an alarm company, you will want to phone them each day to let them know you have work going on during certain hours and that a false alarm is likely. Most systems have a way of taking you off-line for a set number of hours and putting you back on-line when the workers are supposed to be finished for the day. Even with covers and tape the alarm can be triggered.

REMOVING A BEARING WALL

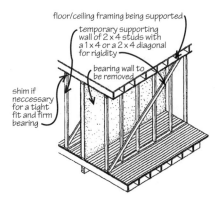

floor/ceiling framing being supported

temporary supporting wall of 2 x 4 studs with a 1 x 4 or a 2 x 4 diagonal for rigidity

bearing wall to be removed

shim if neccessary for a tight fit and firm bearing

If Your Remodeling Begins with Excavation

Unless you're in a new development where construction is ongoing, your yard is going to be popular for the next few days. Your kids will be

The Towel Trick

To preserve unaffected areas during the worst of the demolition, take old towels or sheets, roll them into cylinders, and place them across the bottoms of all nearby doorways. This still allows easy access into the unaffected rooms, while blocking the crevice at the bottom of the door so that you'll have as little extra cleanup as possible.

CONTRACTOR TIP

Protecting Your Priorities

We just finished a job where a beautiful Japanese Maple was located in the middle of the sideyard—directly in the path of the only route the backhoe could use to get into the backyard. We had to present the owner with a choice: He could choose to have the tree removed or we could take special measures, at what would have to be an additional cost. We found an excavator with a particularly narrow backhoe and added in the higher cost of hand carrying out a lot of the debris. The homeowner didn't feel that the additional charge was too prohibitive, so he opted to save the tree.

---

glued to the windows (and you will be, too), and the neighborhood kids and dog-walkers will drift by to watch the hole being dug. There's something really interesting about watching big clawlike equipment at work.

Long before the backhoe arrives to dig your new foundation, you and the contractor should have discussed how the backhoe will get into position to do the work. This is where your yard preparation work comes into play.

Excavation

Before excavation begins the contractor (or a survey team who has been hired for the process) will stake out the measurements of your new addition. This is a good time to pull out your blueprints and walk the area for yourself. Does the addition seem to be placed correctly? If you're concerned, discuss it with your contractor. Don't move the stakes yourself! Also, if you required a variance for your addition—or if your addition puts you very near the point where you might have needed a variance, ask your contractor to double-check all measurements. Building departments can and will ask that structures in violation of local ordinances be torn down and rebuilt.

If the workers are excavating for an addition, they will be digging deep enough for:

- a full basement;
- a crawl space; or
- a cement "slab on grade" (the floor), meaning that there will be no space under the house. In wet areas, such as Florida, where basements would soon become wading pools, the slab on grade is typical.

This stage may be the beginning of the first of the "unexpecteds." Until the crew starts digging, they can't be certain when they will locate soil that is hard enough to build on.

When you talk to people who have had a new foundation dug, almost everyone reports surprise at the size of the hole, that it isn't nearly large enough. Have faith in all the work you've invested in the previous chapters. Just as a room actually looks bigger with furniture so will the hole when the foundation is in.

Preparation for the foundation begins with the footing. This is built by pouring concrete in a trench around the outside perimeter of the construction area. It must always be below whatever your area's frost line is to prevent frost from causing disruption to the house.

Your foundation wall will be built on top of the footing (see illustration below) and may be made of stone, concrete block, brick, or poured concrete (concrete block and poured concrete being the most popular). If your foundation wall (the bearing wall that is designed to hold up the building) is 10 inches wide, then your footing will be double that,

HOW A FOUNDATION WALL IS BUILT

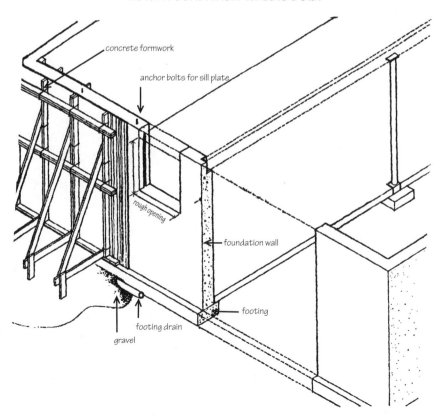

concrete formwork

anchor bolts for sill plate

rough opening

foundation wall

footing

footing drain

gravel

20 inches wide by 10 inches deep. Generally steel reinforcement rods will be used in both the foundation wall and the footings.

After the foundation is installed, the drainage system will be configured. This process involves putting perforated pipe in gravel surrounded by filter fabric and setting it up so that it helps water flow away from your home to a dry well or to low-lying land. Unexpected problems often occur at this stage. For example, they may discover rock that is going to make it expensive to drain as planned. The contractor will be happy to discuss with you what he believes to be the best plan of action. You've lived in the house

FOOTING SIZE

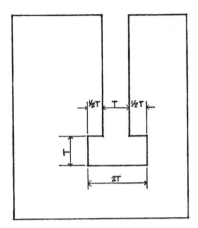

width of footing = 2 x thickness of foundation

depth of footing = thickness of foundation wall

CONCRETE BLOCK FOUNDATION

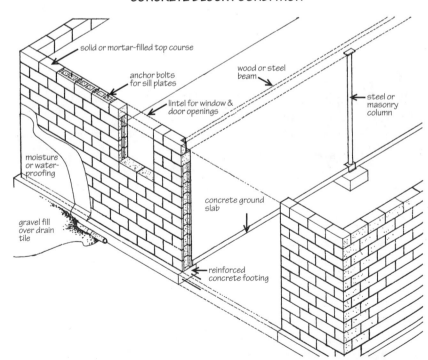

solid or mortar-filled top course

anchor bolts for sill plates

wood or steel beam

lintel for window & door openings

steel or masonry column

moisture or water-proofing

gravel fill over drain tile

concrete ground slab

reinforced concrete footing

for a time and will be able to fill him in on what you've noticed about yard wetness. This will be helpful in coming up with an ultimate solution. Once the drainage system is established, a vapor barrier of plastic and gravel will be created to go under the new addition.

About Inspections

Throughout the process, there will be various inspections required by the building department (see the inspection schedule on page 128). If your project involves a new foundation for an addition, your first inspection will happen once the footing is excavated and formed and before it is in place. If your renovation is interior, the building inspector's first visit will likely be to inspect the framing.

These are important checkpoints in place for your safety. All work that follows a specific inspection must be put on hold until the inspection is completed. A good contractor will know how to schedule the job so that workers can move on to another aspect of your project while waiting the day or two it takes for the building inspector to come give his seal of approval on the work in question.

Becoming Involved

As the early days of your project get underway, you need to establish a system for doing your job, that is, seeing that all is going well. You will need your "homeowner" tools:

- a copy of your plans
- a tape measure (yes, it is worth checking that the measurements are correct)
- a flashlight (for checking at night or going into areas where it is difficult to see)
- your project notebook

Check measurements after the workers leave for the day. Following the carpenter around with a tape measure to double-check his measurements will not be popular with the crew.

Just as you would document discussions at an important business meeting, start documenting discussions with your contractor. In three weeks no one will remember who agreed to be responsible for a specific piece of trim. The cabinetmaker or the contractor? Write it down and mark the date of your discussion.

Each day as you walk through the work area, make notes about items that concern you or that you don't understand. In this early stage, your

Inspections
TYPE	WHAT TO LOOK FOR	TIMING
Footing	Inspect soil to see if it is good "bearing" soil	after excavation, footing formed
	Verify dimensions of footing forms	before you pour footing
	Reinforcement rods in place	
	Bottom of footing below frost line	
Foundation	Drainage in place	after foundation is complete
	foundation as per plans	
	damproofing	before backfilling
Framing	Structural integrity	after work is framed and plumbing, electrical, and HVAC is roughed in
	header, beam, joist sizes	
	fire stopping	
Plumbing Rough	Proper vent and waste lines	after completion of plumbing rough
	Inspector may want water filled in system to test for leaks	sometimes concurrently with framing inspection
	Inspector may want to see water shoot out from roof vent	
Electrical Rough	Rough wiring as per code	after completion of electrical rough
	grounding rods, BX (armored cable) vs. Romex, etc.	
	Sometimes done by a state Underwriter other than local municipality	
HVAC Rough	Installation of ductwork as per code	after completion of HVAC rough
Insulation	Installation as per code	after installation of insulation, before sheetrock
Final/C.O.	Safety Issues	Completion of Project
	railing heights, smoke detectors	
	all working fixtures	
	Area can be used as intended	
	No violations	

Note: Each trade may have separate final inspections checking for code issues and proper installation job will be to look at your plans and the specification for the footings and walls. After the workers have left, go out and look at the foundation. Does everything match up properly?

With the framing stage, you want to be reassured that everything is plumb and level. This will be vital in order for everything else to fit.

Take any and all concerns directly to the contractor. He won't mind explaining what they are doing.

Do not talk to the workers directly about what they are doing and whether they are doing it properly, and do not be accusatory. Chances are that anything you don't understand is perfectly correct and can be easily explained.

The Framing

Once the foundation elements are taken care of, the framing will begin. Sometimes a specialty crew will arrive for this work, other times the contractor's workers will do it. It's an exciting stage, because in a matter of days you'll see room outlines and begin to get a sense of what your new addition will look like!

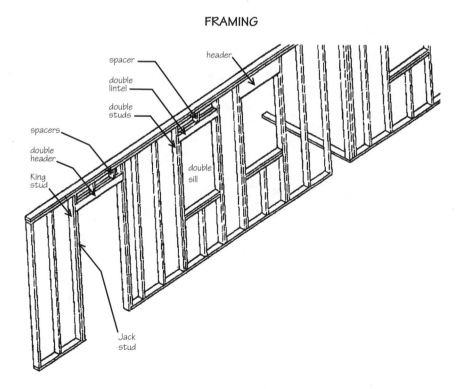

FRAMING

WOOD JOIST FLOOR SYSTEM

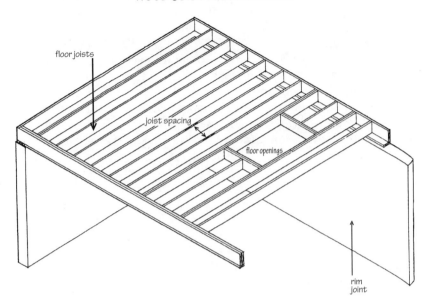

floor joists

joist spacing

floor openings

rim joint

Your foundation hole will be backfilled once the first floor deck is secured to help reduce stress on the foundation wall. The backhoe may remain on site or will return in anticipation of this additional job.

If your project involves remodeling existing space, you'll also see the framers who will create a frame for the interior space according to your plans.

The Roof

When the framers finish, the roofers arrive. Depending on your selection, they will install a roof made of clay tile, slate, metal, or the most frequently used: fiberglass asphalt shingle. The roof of the addition will probably have to join adjacent roofing materials, and the old and new are woven together to create a waterproof covering.

Roofers also install counter flashing, chimney flashing, roof-edge flashing, gutters, and leaders.

On the Job Communication

As day one gets underway, you'll begin to get a sense of how best to communicate. If you leave for work early one day will your note be read? If they leave before you get home at the end of the day, will they communicate with you about any sort of problem that occurred? Until the

ROOF FRAMING

project gets rolling, a lot of these things will be unsaid. Here are some suggestions that will put you on the right foot with the contractor:

1. Communicate directly with the contractor or his foreman. Other than greeting the workers or talking a moment about the weather, direct communication with the crew or with the subcontractors is inappropriate.
2. Find out what the best way to reach the contractor is now that the job is starting. He may provide you with a home phone number or a beeper number for after-hours emergencies.
3. In a real emergency, call 911.
4. Be open in your communication. Kevin says: "Tell me what you like. Tell me what you don't like. If something displeases you and you speak up right away, the situation may be easily solved. If you wait, the situation may become worse—and harder to solve."
5. Test out note-writing or lists as a method of communication. If you can hand the contractor a list of your concerns, it is easier for both of you to run through the items and check them off. Some people are note phobic and this will never work, but, for those who respond, it gives you the opportunity to get through things quickly and easily.
6. Don't socialize. They are in your home to work, and it's important that they have the time to do so.
7. Set up a communication system that works. Sometimes one spouse refuses to be a message-bearer because it's the other one's project. This is a family communication problem that will slow the project.

The Importance of Relaxation and Trust

Assuming that your honeymoon gets off to a normal start, your job is to relax and leave the work to the contractor and her crew. There are all types of clients, and I can tell you about a few "types" who may mean well but they actually slow a project down:

- Remember that when this was just a blueprint, you **wanted** this job done—you invited us in to do it. Sometimes we arrive on a job and it is clear that the family finds us annoying and disruptive. Welcome us in and let us work steadily and quickly; we'll try to be out of your way as soon as possible.
- Benefit from our experience. One woman was a researcher by profession, so when it came to renovating her home, she researched. She presented us with photocopied pages on all types of installations and work to be done, but the occasion when she really created havoc was the day we re-asphalted her driveway. She was absolutely certain that the fellow doing the work had gotten the temperature of the asphalt wrong so she kept calling to him over the roar of the steamroller. He had been putting down asphalt for nearly 20 years,

and he was absolutely certain he had gotten it right. We finished the job without her getting flattened under the roller, but it was close. If she'd had concerns, she should have discreetly discussed them with me. Interference like this does nothing but slow a job and reduce the likelihood that the worker is going to go the extra mile to make certain that your job is done just right.

- Remember that we're experts. If we recommend that a wall needs to come down or that the wiring needs to be changed, you needn't look for three other people to tell you this. You've hired experts to take care of your job, so now that we're here you will benefit by listening to us.
- Hire an honest contractor with good references and then treat him like a professional. Pay on time and abide by what you've all agreed is a fair payment schedule. Sometimes when I give someone a bill, they'll explain that money will be forthcoming shortly: "I'll transfer some money tomorrow . . ." is something I hear frequently. Most of the money I collect goes to pay expenses—the next materials order needed for your job or the salaries of the workers who are at your home. If

The Importance of Relaxation and Trust
(continued)

I have to start worrying about where I'm going to get the money to pay for the next stages of your job, that's going to prevent me from focusing on getting your job done right.

- Please don't scream at any of us. Family stress can be high during a remodeling job, but there is no need to yell and scream and berate the workers. If there's a problem, tell me. We'll do everything in our power to work it out.

One of the most upsetting incidents my company ever experienced happened on an extremely hot day and involved a husband and wife who didn't agree on the importance of the project. The job was just beginning, and the temperature was in the mid-90s and so was the humidity. We had been instructed to access the worksite on one side of the house, but with the husband's approval we were bringing some extraordinarily long beams to the back of the house on the "wrong"—but by far the more convenient—side of the house. Well, marital communications evidently hadn't been good that day, and my workers, lugging 800-pound beams in the scorching heat, were treated to a royal dressing down by the wife. With her nonstop screaming, my foreman couldn't even explain. Unnerved by her behavior, his only thought was to leave the area and to call me to tell me what was happening. Hopping into his truck that was loaded high with plywood for the job, he failed to see a Mercedes turning into the homeowner's driveway, and backed right into it. Had the wife come out and calmly asked for an explanation, we could have explained how the size of beam prevented us from accessing the backyard from the direction discussed, and we could have informed her that her husband had given his "okay." The afternoon could have concluded with hot, exhausted workers who looked forward to returning to the job after the weekend. As it was, we ended with one irate homeowner, two damaged cars, and a host of workers who could hardly be expected to give 125% to a woman who had called them every name in the book.

Ask for an explanation and if you're still angry, talk to the contractor. When tempers cool, the two of you can work things out. It's virtually impossible to mend relations if you've also screamed at five or six workers who were just doing what they were told.

8. Do the workers speak English? If not, ask your contractor who will be there to deal with unexpected problems that arise. One Connecticut homeowner had a tile delivery from Oregon that had to be sent back to Oregon because there was no foreman on the job at the time it arrived. The workers did not speak English and payment had not been made, so the shipment went back and got lost along the way. "Our job was held up for two months while the company relocated the tile all because the workers couldn't understand what the trucker's problem was."

End of Day Ritual

This is the time to establish what will be the end of day ritual for the workers:

Are all open areas tarped? This may be necessary for a degree of security. If the tarping is primarily for protection from weather, your expectations should be modified by your area of the country. If you live in a dry climate where rainfall is a rarity, then the workers needn't tarp every night unless rain is expected.

Is the house secure and, if necessary, have they locked up for the night? If they have broken through existing walls, discuss with the contractor exactly how "lock up" is going to be achieved.

Has the power, heat, and hot water been restored?
What could be more annoying than to discover that the workers have left and you have no heat or hot water? (It happens.)

Has a general cleanup been performed? As you interviewed contractors, you should have discussed expectations of cleanup, and these are the days when you'll see it put into operation. Keep in mind that a cleanup that would pass a white-glove inspection isn't cost-effective. However, your family certainly shouldn't be stepping through dust piles and loose nails.

Have all power tools been unplugged and stored away?

What If There Is No Honeymoon Period?

In interviews for this book, we heard the same advice offered again and again: If your contractor gets off to a shaky start, cancel the contract **now**. Considering the distance you have left to go, there should be no second chance.

One family rented a vacation home so they could vacate their home during demolition. The first concerned call came from a neighbor who reported that the cement truck ignored the homeowner's driveway (which would have led the truck to an acceptable spot for delivery) and drove right up the front lawn, leaving six-inch-deep ruts in the lawn. The second call came from the contractor when he sheepishly reported that he had failed to tarp up the house for the night and a violent rainstorm had saturated their baby grand piano.

"We still didn't get it," says the homeowner. "We tried to continue working with him, but it was one bad thing after another, and we finally had to fire him."

Cut your losses. If things don't get off to a good start, trust your instincts and get out. Starting over with someone new is not ideal, but working with someone who has shown bad judgment from the start may lead to pain far greater than starting over.

Homeowner Checklist

- Discuss with the contractor what arrangement will be made for debris.
- Ask to be introduced to the various workers as they arrive.
- Do your part to clear the work space (see chapter 8.)
- Order all homeowner-provided items.
- Be certain that the workers have covered all smoke alarms.
- Notify the alarm company daily that you have workers in the house and that false alarms are possible.
- Each morning stuff towels along the bottom of doors into unaffected rooms.
- Walk the excavated area to check the location of the addition.
- Begin documenting conversations you have with your contractor. In your project notebook keep track of any changes in responsibility, and any new decisions you discuss.
- Set up a system for regular communication. Does the contractor respond well to notes or lists? Is there a time to meet and talk regularly?
- Ask that at the end of the day the workers go through the following checklist:
  - Are all open areas tarped?
  - Is the house secure?
  - Has the power, heat, and hot water been restored?
  - Have they cleaned up?
  - Have all power tools been unplugged and all tools stored away?

Chapter 10

More Noise, (Slightly) Less Dirt: The Arrival of the Tradespeople

You've been through a lot with the demolition or excavation and framing. It's been dirty, loud, and disruptive, but you've made it. You're used to the workers arriving at 8 A.M., breaking for lunch around noon (giving you momentary peace), and putting everything away by 4 P.M. With this schedule, you're able to get the house clean enough for the kids to settle in to do homework and for you to figure out what to do about dinner. It's not fun, but you're getting there.

But here come the tradespeople (heating and air-conditioning experts, plumbers, electricians, and Sheetrockers), the people your contractor has subcontracted some of the work to. The day before they are to start, the contractor pulls you aside: "My plumber likes to start at 7 A.M., and the electrician usually starts late but likes to work straight through. You don't mind if he stays until 8 P.M. or so? It will let us get the job done faster . . ."

Well, what are you going to say? "No, I want the job to stretch out as long as possible"? (Obviously, if you just can't manage the 7 A.M. start you'll have to say so, but accommodating the workers as much as you can will help speed the job along.) If you set too many barriers, then the "best plumber in town" or "the only plumber the contractor trusts" will find a house where they will let him start at 7 A.M. and finish at 3 P.M. So keep the door open, don't lock up midday, and the parade of workers will continue.

It's a new stage of the work—new people, new rhythm.

Maintaining Communication

Communicating well with your contractor is more important now than ever. New crews are arriving, and careful supervision by the contractor or his foreman is critical. That's what you're paying him for.

Before the tradespeople begin, remind the contractor of some of the family practices that they've begun to take for granted and ask him to communicate them to the group that's due to arrive. Your list might include items such as these:

- The cat should not be let out of the upstairs bedroom while the workers are around.
- The back gate should be kept closed at all times.
- Workers should not park so that they block the family car from leaving the driveway.

Communicating with your contractor remains important. While you'll probably talk informally each day, set a time to meet more formally once each week. This gives you both an opportunity to catch up. The contractor can fill you in on who should be coming that week, and you can review with him some of the items that concern you at the time.

As they rip out wires and pipes in preparation for the new installations that will be made, there will continue to be unexpected occurrences. Availability and fast decision-making on your part will be helpful to the workers if and when these situations occur.

The Stages of Work

There are basically three sets of tradespeople who will be involved at this point: the electrician, the plumber, and the heating, ventilation and air conditioning team (HVAC). (Plumbers often do the heating work if ducts don't need to be installed for forced air or air conditioning. This narrows your group of tradespeople to two.)

Three stages of work must be performed by each group, and they must be done in a carefully orchestrated sequence. Occasionally stages one and two are performed in a single visit, but since there is an order to the work, they must often spread the job out over three separate visits.

Demolition stage. This is different from the demolition you've just been through. The work involves closing down or tearing out the appropriate mechanisms. The plumber may cap off pipes so that a fixture can be relocated; the electrician may shut off electricity to parts of the house so that the electrical work can be done.

The "rough-in" stage. During this time the workers put in the behind-the-wall elements according to your plans. The heating and air-conditioning ducts will be put in place, and, if you're relocating the kitchen sink, the plumber will install the pipes so that the new sink can be located where you want it. The electrician will put in all the wires she needs for the new lights you've specified.

The rough-in work occurs when the walls are open and framed and the place is weathertight. It is performed in the following order:

- The mechanical workers, or "tin knockers" as they are called, will come in and install the duct work needed for the heating and air-conditioning systems. There is the least flexibility in their installation, because their materials are the biggest and bulkiest. For that reason, they are first on the scene.

- Coming in behind the tin knockers are the plumbers who will run pipes through the necessary areas.
- The third group to arrive will be the electricians whose wires are the easiest to wrap around and through tight spaces.

Finish work. This occurs much later. The tradespeople come back and make their systems operable. Radiators are installed. The electrician puts in light fixtures and switches, and the plumber hooks up faucets to his behind-the-wall piping systems.

In other words, you'll be seeing a lot of these people over a prolonged period of time.

Living through This Stage

First, if you don't know the locations of the main shut-offs of power and water find out now. If anything goes wrong at this stage, you might need to know this quickly.

Discuss with your contractor the inconveniences you are likely to experience and for how long. Throughout this stage, power and water may have to be shut down periodically. If you're at home most of the time, it is reasonable to request that they notify you a few minutes in advance that something must be shut down. That lets you get water you need or relocate to a part of the house where the power will be unaffected.

On some occasions, the workers may need to disconnect power or water indefinitely. If the water leaves you with one working bathroom instead of two for a couple of days that's probably manageable, if it leaves you with no working bathroom it's not. Talk to them about how this problem can be solved.

When it comes to power, electricity can always be rigged but at a cost. One family was remodeling their kitchen and the power to one section of the house had to be off for about a week, leaving the daughter's bedroom in darkness. The family was given a choice: Should the workers take the time to rewire the bedroom lights or not? Because their daughter could do homework elsewhere in the house, the family decided to have the workers keep going. The week passed uneventfully, and the situation was not what the family will remember as a major inconvenience. (What they do remember vividly is doing dinner dishes in the basement sink, which necessitated going out the front door and around to the back door since the stairs were inaccessible due to the remodeling.)

Heating, Ventilation, and Air Conditioning

This is your last opportunity to rethink this system. Talk to your contractor about anything that will need to be changed based on any surprises found during demolition. Is there still space for the radiator you had slated for the bathroom? If not, what is the solution?

Review the plans with the contractor again to consider how the duct work will be run. Is all still on schedule? The location where the mechanical workers put the ducts will lead the way for the plumbing pipes and the electrical wires. Now that the framing is done, will any main beams be in the way? Does anything need to be changed? Ask the contractor to point out how the ducts will run. That way you'll be able to check that the fellow who arrives the next morning follows the plans and doesn't decide to take a shorter route from point A to point B.

Ask, too, about repairs. If this system goes down, are they doing all they can to make it easy to repair later on? Particularly if you're tying into an old system, the work must be done thoughtfully and carefully to make certain that problems later on will be easy to rectify. If you're installing steam heat or hot water, the piping should route back to the base rather frequently. That way if the system has to be drained for any reason, it will be easier to do.

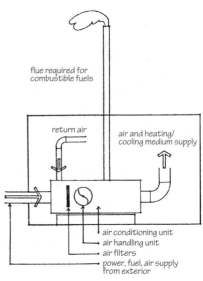

HVAC SYSTEMS

flue required for combustible fuels

return air

air and heating/ cooling medium supply

air conditioning unit
air handling unit
air filters
power, fuel, air supply from exterior

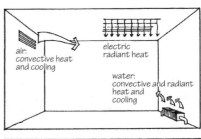

air: convective heat and cooling

electric radiant heat

water: convective and radiant heat and cooling

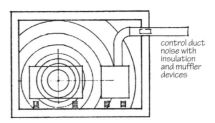

control duct noise with insulation and muffler devices

isolate noise - by distance (location)
- with mass (enclosure)
- by use of vibration control devices (installation)

HVAC SYSTEMS

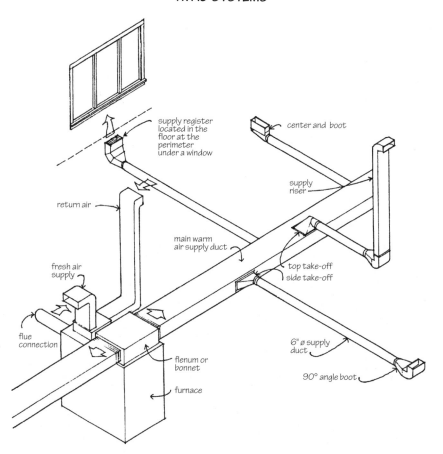

supply register located in the floor at the perimeter under a window

center and boot

supply riser

return air

main warm air supply duct

fresh air supply

top take-off

side take-off

flue connection

6" ø supply duct

flenum or bonnet

90° angle boot

furnace

Here Come the Plumbers

Water is a treacherous element. If released unexpectedly, it can cause a major flood in your home. If released slowly over time, it can cause dry rot where wood is alternately wet and then dry. Ultimately, it causes a weakening of the wood and the eventual collapse of part of your house. (Take it from me. We never thought to ask where all the water that kept leaking in a window during major storms was going. We found out one night when I was doing the dishes and half the kitchen ceiling collapsed.)

Obviously, you want an excellent plumber. He should be licensed and well respected by your contractor. If the contractor urges you to wait until a certain fellow is available, it's worth waiting. Everything has to vent properly, drain properly, and mix into the original system properly.

One on-the-spot evaluation that should be made by the plumber and the contractor concerns the condition of your current pipes. If the walls are open and the contractor and plumber show you reason for replacement, do it now. Also, ask about the soldering—pipe soldering used to be done with a lead substance, something everyone wants out of their home now. If you have lead-soldered pipes, now is the time to have them replaced.

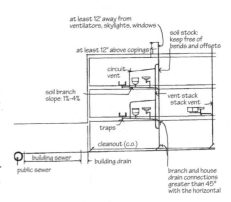

If you're adding a spa or an oversized tub, talk to the contractor and plumber about the base. Often these should be put on a platform to give additional support and to better distribute the weight.

Check with the contractor about whether or not the pipes will be pressure-tested. (A special gauge that checks pipes should be used; simply filling the system with water isn't enough as it may take time for a small leak to appear.) Tell him you want all pipes pressure-tested and double-checked. This will prevent pipes from leaking later on.

All gas pipes should be tested as well. This is required in new construction, but sometimes workers cut corners in remodeling. Don't let them.

ELECTRICAL WIRING

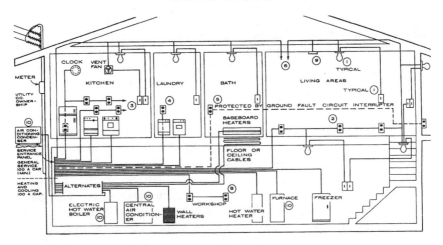

The Electricians

With all of today's new gadgetry and appliances, lots of wiring is a necessity. Ask for separate wires and breakers for major appliances so that you don't blow a circuit every time you vacuum. Many local codes require separate breakers for each kitchen appliance, and it's a good idea.

Remember to request a dedicated outlet for computers and wall air conditioners.

Also, if plastic outlet boxes are being used instead of metal, each one will need to be grounded separately. Be sure your contractor checks for this.

Handling Worker Complaints with Diplomacy

Inevitably, you will get worker complaints. With some personality types, a small problem will occur and become a major roadblock, or one of the crew members will want to be a "hero" and save your project from sure disaster.

As the fatherly plumber explains how "these young fellows just don't understand plumbing the way they ought to and that he's really going to have to rework everything," you may be inclined to comfort him with "do what you think is best." Resist this inclination! Instead, listen carefully. Then speak to your contractor. He will be able to check on the validity of the claims and correct what needs to be corrected.

You've spent a lot of time thinking and planning for this remodeling job. Don't be swayed by a worker who arrives and sees only one part of the picture. He may have seen your blueprints, but he will have only studied the part involving his job. Perhaps you and your designer had discussed a Stage Two remodeling project you might do in a few years. What the tradesperson sees as a "major obstacle" may be laying the groundwork for this eventual project.

Insist that they follow the plans unless you and the contractor (or you, the designer, and contractor) agree on a new course of action. "Doing what they think is best" will all too often be what is good—or easy—for them, not what is good for you.

As more and more people come to your home (what they call the job site), you will run across some you dislike. The electrician may be a joker and a fun guy to have around, but the plumber may be an eternal complainer. You walk a fine line here. There's a limit to what you should have to put up with, but vent your irritation on the contractor, not the tradesperson.

Why? Because you want them to give their best. A tradesperson can do their job well or poorly, and poorly can hurt you a lot. Especially at

HOMEOWNER TIP

Keeping the Big Picture in Mind

Mistakes will happen. You'll find that home remodeling will show how very human we are. If five people are involved in the ordering and installation of a particular item, then you have five opportunities for something to go wrong. What matters is how the issue is resolved.

Fixing doesn't always have to involve tearing out and starting over. Although having them rip out something you don't like is your right, it may not always be the best solution. Perhaps there is something the following sub or one of the contractor's people can do to fix what went wrong. Consider whether there are alternatives

before you start talking "rip out," which takes extra time and may not be worth it in the long run.

When we were redoing one of our bathrooms, we noticed that a new worker was sent in to do some of the framing. A few days later, one of the carpenters I knew was considered one of their best arrived, closed the bathroom door and proceeded to do a day's additional work on what I thought was a framed bathroom. The first fellow had not managed to get the raised ceiling correct, and Bill was sent in to correct it. There was no need to discuss this with me, so long as it was taken care of.

the in-the-wall stage, a pipe that isn't joined perfectly can lead to a slow leak that can cause great damage later on when your renovation is finished. Let them do their work, complaining or joking, and continue your communication with the contractor.

The Homeowner Patrol

As each worker completes the rough-in stage, you have some work to do.

After everyone has left for the evening, take your blueprints into the work area and check to see that everything seems to be in the right place.

Is the piping for the toilet where you expected it to be? What about the sink? Check these carefully. If you're doubtful, talk to the contractor. Brenner Builders had to totally rip out a marble bath (walls and floor) because the fixtures, even though they were placed according to plan, were misplaced for optimum use. The job was 90% complete, the marble and fixtures were in, when the homeowner pointed out that the bidet was seated too close to the whirlpool for practical usage. They rebuilt the bathroom—removing marble, redoing plumbing, taking up the floor—in order to get everything shifted around. It would have been faster and cheaper to make these changes during the rough-in stage.

How are the locations of the radiators and the air diffusers for the air conditioning? Think again about how the room will be used. Now that you see it framed do you still envision the furniture arrangement you planned? Did "surprises" discovered during construction alter anything that might make a difference? You don't want the air diffusers under pieces of furniture or right by doorways. This is your last chance to verify that all is as it should be. A problem discovered now will be a nuisance to fix but nothing compared to what will happen if it's discovered after the walls are closed.

Double-check that all plumbing pipes placed on exterior walls are insulated. Frozen pipes in the winter are no fun and are extremely hazardous to the health of your house. (A burst pipe can lead to a whole new series of renovations.)

Walk into each room and consider the electrical placement. As you come to each doorway, consider whether the light switch is conveniently placed. If you have two entrances to the room, you may want to consider a three-way switch where the overhead light can be turned on or off from each entrance. Now is the time to think through any changes you decide are necessary and make them.

This is also the time when any of the accessory wiring you've opted for (in-wall speaker wiring, phone wiring, alarm boxes, exterior motion detectors, timers, outdoor lights, or computer cables) should be installed. Check with the contractor to be certain that these elements have been provided for.

You or the contractor should also be in touch with the alarm company. At this point they will need to come do their wiring.

Compare your plans with all the work that is going to be buried in the walls. Ask your contractor to point out any place where they couldn't go according to plan. This change should be documented on your plans so that you'll have an accurate blueprint for pulling wires through once the Sheetrock is up. And later on, if anything ever has to be repaired, your blueprint will be accurate. Some people even photograph the walls while they are open to provide full documentation.

If for any reason you've lost faith in the contractor or were uncomfortable with the tradesmen, hire an independent inspector to come through at this time. Schedule this visit for a time when no workers are around, because this idea will not be popular with your contractor or crew. Ultimately, it's your home and if you have any doubts, you ought to get reassurance (or find that you have trouble) at this time.

CONTRACTOR TIP

Dominos in Action

We were excavating for a new addition to a house when we discovered that the rock could not be safely excavated as deeply as the plans indicated. The homeowners wanted a full basement, so the solution was to raise the new part of the house by eight inches, giving them the full basement and lifting everything else. This was the beginning of the domino effect.

The "new" job required 100 cubic yards of additional fill; the patio stairs now required an extra step; a retainer wall was needed at the site of the garage entrance; and we had to go to the zoning board to ask for a variance because the house would exceed local height limits. We spent an additional $8,000 and a lot of extra time all because of that first domino.

The Domino Effect

At any time during home remodeling, changes can and will occur. Remember the domino effect. If one thing changes, other things may as well.

After "How much will this cost?", the most important words you can utter are "Will this change anything else?" Whenever a change occurs or the contractor discusses with you something that couldn't fully be completed according to plan, pull out your copy of the blueprints. Ask for an explanation of the change, and then talk about what else will be affected.

The Number One Construction Accident

Once the rough-in plumbing work has been completed, it's time for the tub or the shower body to arrive. Great, you say. Not so great, really.

Though the placement must be made at this stage, there are still so many workers coming in and out of the house that your tub or shower body is in great danger of being scratched or damaged in some way. (This happens frequently and is totally preventable.) Here's what to do:

1. Insist that the contractor bring in a new drop cloth and use it to cover the tub, draping it inside and around the edges. Make certain it's new or completely clean. You don't want bits of cement chips dropping into your tub, only to be ground into the finish at some later stage.

CONTRACTOR TIP

Well-Intentioned Advice from Friends and Other Communication Issues

About this time, you will have acquired a lot of advice from friends and possibly from Bob Vila.

Some of the comments you hear stir up issues that can be explained, so be sure to give me that opportunity. Your home will be a hodgepodge if you alter your plans every time someone makes a remark.

Other comments—particularly from relatives who are in the business—are more difficult. "My cousin is a window installer, and he says the windows should have been. . . ." In response to a comment such as this I refrain from telling clients they should have hired their cousin. Where was he when the walls were open and we were coping with an old house that was out of plumb? He likely would have made the decisions we did if he'd been there from the beginning. You hired me; now trust me to do the best job for you.

As for Bob Vila, his methods are greatly simplified and his circumstances are television perfect. It's fine to keep asking us questions, but trust us when we tell you that even Bob Vila would have done it this way had he been here.

This is also a stage in which the homeowner starts playing us against each other. Don't try telling the electrician that I've authorized that he put in several new outlets at no charge. Obviously, this deception will come out in the long run.

Talk to me, complain to me, keep me informed. Don't let a problem fester. If we discuss it now, it can probably be corrected quickly. One time a homeowner kept screaming at me, and I couldn't understand why she was that upset about what happened. It turned out that several days before one of the men used one of her good towels to clean up. If she had asked us to replace the towel, it would have been far less emotional than venting her irritation on some other small detail. Marital tension may also be high about now. Don't draw us into disputes, and don't ask me to take sides. I will give my opinion freely if it concerns value or product quality. But don't ask me if one is prettier than another, and don't ask me to side with you or your spouse.

---

2. Ask that they cut a new piece of plywood to cover the entire top of the tub so that there is a layer of hard protection over the surface.

Shower bodies are usually packed in foam and wrapped in plastic; ask that the workers leave on all possible protective wrap.

If you have read this section
belatedly and your tub or shower is
already damaged, then you have the
right to ask for a new one. However,
most homeowners aren't up to the
thought of the tub being uprooted
from the almost-complete bathroom
and a new one put in. The contractor can hire a firm to come in and
do some cosmetic work to repair the
tub, but the results probably won't
be perfect.

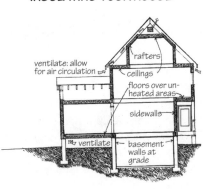

INSULATING YOUR HOUSE

Inspection Time

Soon your house will be ready for a local inspection. Generally a framing inspection will be conducted concurrently with a mechanical,
plumbing, and electrical inspection.

Once the inspections are complete, insulation is the next step. In all
likelihood, the materials will be delivered a few days ahead of time. Keep
the kids away from it. Most insulation used today is a petroleum-based
product. It's smelly, and it itches when it comes in contact with the skin.

It's time for another homeowner inspection (after hours, of course).
As you go through the rooms you want to see that there are no visible
gaps between pieces of insulation. There should also be no exterior construction material visible from the inside. Also, double-check with your
contractor that any fire-stop or sound-proof materials have been
installed before the drywall. Sound proofing might go around a home
office, a psychiatrist's consultation room, a family room where the kids
are loud, etc. Fire-stopping is installed around rooms like the boiler
room and between floors to prevent the spread of fire.

A Contractor's Plea Regarding Homeowner-Provided Items

If you have agreed to provide anything—from cabinetry to light fixtures
to special knobs—be certain that you have them on hand now.

As soon as you receive the item (whether it's a single cabinet or 24
knobs), go over each carefully, and ask the contractor to inspect it as
well. He may spot imperfections that you miss. If something is imperfect
and has to be sent back, talk to your contractor. Even if you've ordered
the item, perhaps there is an insider's way to expedite the return.

If the item in question isn't on hand when the crew needs it, you
will all be sorely disappointed. A knob, of course, will create only a

minor inconvenience, but if it's something major, like cabinetry or a shower body that must be buried behind the walls, then it can start off a string of delays that wreak havoc with the schedule.

We just completed a job in which some missing cabinets delayed the finish by two months. We'd been working on the house for about eight months, with major renovations throughout. The owners had special kitchen cabinets they wanted and ordered the cabinets themselves. They came in on time, but with the wrong hinges. Our first response was, "Well, these things happen. We'll switch the hinges as we install them."

On closer examination, it was apparent that the screw holes for the two styles of hinges were different. Since no one wanted patched screw holes on the front panels of new lacquer cabinets, there was nothing to do but send back the cabinets, drawing the finish work in the kitchen to a screeching halt for what was to be a minimum of a six-week wait.

We set up a temporary kitchen arrangement for the family so that they could move in, but six weeks later we had to return to install the new cabinetry—providing them with a mess they did not intend to live through, and creating a scheduling delay for us that was a nightmare.

Few homeowners realize that when one major element goes badly, everything else has to be rescheduled. All the other finish workers—the plumber, the electrician, the carpenters, the tiler)—that were to come in after the cabinetry was installed on this particular job, had to scramble

TAPING SHEETROCK

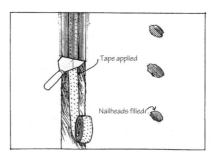

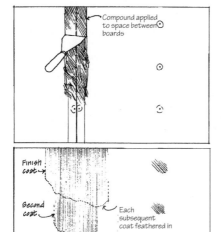

TAPING SHEETROCK

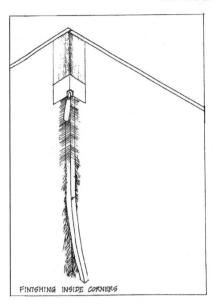

FINISHING INSIDE CORNERS

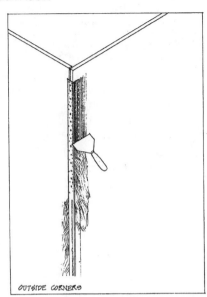

OUTSIDE CORNERS

for other jobs since they couldn't do the job they intended at the expected time. Then, when it was time for them to come back, they were booked with jobs they had to take to fill in. As a result, it took even more time to get everyone rescheduled to finish up.

While some delays are inevitable—and mistakes do happen—you will do yourself a service by taking all possible measures to see that you will have the correct items in hand:

1. **Double-check what's being ordered.** At a showroom, ask to see the order form and compare it with the catalog number of the item you want. If you're working with an artisan, ask him or her to double-check all measurements in the field to make certain there are no variations, misunderstandings, or mistakes.

2. **Follow up appropriately.** If they say, "two to four weeks," start calling at the end of the second week.

3. **Conduct in-progress inspections, if called for.** If your cabinetmaker is trying to match a special stain, arrange to see it before the cabinet is delivered. Or if you're purchasing a special type of marble, you'll want to inspect and handpick what is to be installed.

If you've taken these measures, you'll have done all that is possible to assure that you will get what you need when it's needed.

Rocking along with the Sheetrockers

Experience has shown that there's something about this stage of a project where everyone's patience begins to wear thin. One of my foremen describes it as the not-enough-Prozac stage. By this time there has been a lot of action on a project. You may have had a dozen people or more in and out of your house during the last few weeks, and it's getting tiring. Maybe they were supposed to finish before the holidays and now it looks like you'll have to have Thanksgiving in a tarp-draped dining room—not the end of the world—but not the first choice either. Buck up, you've got a new group coming through.

Sometimes the contractor's own people will put up the Sheetrock (the wallboard used these days instead of plaster). Other times, specialty crews will come through. They arrive with their own music and maybe some footwear your kids will be dying to try out (to speed up parts of the job that would otherwise require a ladder, the workers wear stilts that fasten directly to the foot, leaving their hands free.) They'll clatter through your house in no time.

Three types of Sheetrock are used.

1. Standard Sheetrock is one-half-inch thick and is generally used on walls and ceilings. A slightly thicker version of this is fire-rated and used for boiler rooms, garages, and anywhere there is a live flame.
2. Green board is a moisture-resistant Sheetrock and is used where there is expected to be a heavy moisture buildup, such as in bathrooms. It can only be used on walls because of its excessive weight.
3. Wonder Board is used for shower stall and bathtub areas. It is a cementitious tile-backer and is used only with tile or marble. It is the most water-resistant kind of wallboard. Some tilers insist on installing Wonder Board themselves. Others will be content with letting your Sheetrockers put it up for you.

Sheetrock will arrive at your home on a big flatbed truck with a boom arm. Because the pieces are so large, it is sometimes delivered through a window rather than trying to bring it up a stairway. This, of course, will bring the neighborhood kids back to see what you're doing now.

Ceilings will be placed first, then the walls. Sheetrock should be screwed in, rather than nailed, because nails often pop out as the house settles. As they work, the sheetrockers should be marking all the places where they are hiding pipes and electrical work.

After the Sheetrock is up, the walls generally require three or four coats of tape and joint compound. This is when the Sheetrock stage can become messy. The better the Sheetrocker, the less need for overspackling, and the less need for heavy sanding. With luck, you'll survive this stage with a minimum of dust.

After the primer coat of paint, there will be one final inspection of the Sheetrock seams, generally performed by the painter.

Now we come to the most important and rewarding part of the job, the finishing phase.

Homeowner Checklist

- Remind the contractor to tell this new group of workers about any special considerations such as keeping the gate to the back-yard closed, not blocking driveway access to the garage, etc.
- Discuss potential inconveniences such as when and if power or water may be turned off.
- Remember that any complaints you have about this new group of workers should be made to the contractor.
- Conduct your own after-hours inspection regarding placement of the systems.
- Contact the alarm company to let them know you're ready for them to do their wiring.
- Keep in mind the domino effect. If one thing changes, ask the contractor if anything else will need to be altered.
- If your remodeling involves a new bathtub or shower body, be certain that the workers take measures to protect them.
- Right after the building inspection occurs, the insulation will be installed. Do another after-hours inspection to be certain that all new areas are well insulated.
- After the Sheetrockers leave, your new walls should be marked to show the locations of all pipes and wires. Make certain that they are.
- Be sure that any and all homeowner-provided items arrive on time.

Chapter 11

Patience Is a Virtue: The Finishing Phase

"Our project was going like gangbusters!" says Trish Anderson. "We were delighted with the contractor, with the crew, with everything. They had the addition closed up by Halloween, and we thought for sure they'd be gone before Christmas. Then everything slowed down. When I came home, there were always workers here, but I could rarely tell exactly what they had done that day. The finishing work just took a lot longer than we expected. It was mid-January before we said good-bye."

"Why is it taking so long?" everyone asks during the finishing phase. In fact, finish work, often only 10% of the job, can take up to 50% of the entire construction time!

What Happens during the Finishing Phase?

As the finish phase begins, your remodeled or added space will begin to look like a home. The Sheetrock is up and has had its last coat, and the work of putting the finishes on top of and around the Sheetrock will now get underway:

1. Floor surfaces—wood, tile, slate, linoleum—go down.
2. The trim work (the wooden frames around windows, and the crown and base moldings) will be completed.
3. Doors will be hung and trimmed.
4. Wall tile in bathroom or kitchen will be set.
5. The millwork (custom cabinetry) is installed and any wainscoting is put in place.
6. Each of the subcontractors may have a "finishing" aspect to his job, too. Faucet handles must be installed, radiator covers put in place, and outlet covers added.

Everything must be done in sequence, which can sometimes cause delays. The baseboards can't be put in until the floors are done; the crown molding must be in place before the seven-foot bookcases are placed—everything must proceed logically and in order. If one part remains undone, all other workers must wait.

As this work gets underway, you will probably notice a different atmosphere. Even if some of the carpenters are the same people who did your framing they are now finishers, and, as the job dictates, they are more careful and cautious.

You may want to hurry them along but resist. This is the phase of the work that really makes or breaks a job. How the cabinetry looks, whether or not the kitchen tile is straight, and the color match between old flooring and new flooring are the types of things you (and your guests) will notice first. For that reason, be patient and respectful. You want them to work slowly and carefully now.

Just when You Thought Things Were Getting Better . . .

The demolition dust clouds have subsided, you're no longer tripping over 2 × 4s laid out for framing, and the stacks of insulation are gone. With great pleasure, your in-house mess has diminished and is more

WINDOW DETAIL

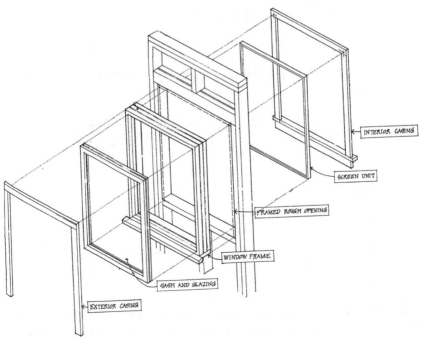

DOOR FRAMING

To retain a close fit, nail from the top. For butt joint, nail from the side. Predrill hole to prevent splitting of wood.

¼" Reveal (see drawing below)

Corner block

A plinth block may be used to terminate the side casing

Mitered joints must be used to join molded or shaped casing trim.

Butt joints can be used for square-cut casing trim.

A corner block can be used to join more complex casing trim shapes.

Wall framing

Side jamb

Stop

Hollow back of trim allows for slight irregularities in wall surface.

Nail to wall framing (stud)

Nail to door frame (jamb)

Space each pair of nails 12" to 16" o.c.

¼" Reveal (set back from face of jamb)

likely to be small piles of sawdust in specific work areas. But wait. You're not finished yet. There are still the floor finishes and possibly some tile cutting as well.

If you're putting in hardwood floors, things are going to get worse before they get better. Dust from the sanding will permeate all but the farthest closets, and the odor from the stain and polyurethane is noxious.

Most families move out for a few days at this stage, partly because of the dust and the smell but mainly because you can't walk on the floor

INSIDER'S TIP

"Five Guys Were Here—What Did They Do?"

The changes you see at this stage will be subtle. All of the work must be performed carefully with craftsmanlike attention to detail. Some of your workers even consider themselves artisans. Observe as the tiler plans out the floor design in the bathroom, and notice the carpenter working on the new mantelpiece. A staircase builder may take several days to set up a job, laying out all his tools and materials as carefully as a surgeon prepares for an operation.

They are working hard. It's just not as dramatic as pouring a foundation or carrying out garbage containers full of disappearing debris.

for at least 24 hours. Depending on the area of the house affected (often the hallways), this may prohibit anyone from moving around the house.

Tile cutting, if it needs to be done inside the house, is similar to the mess created by hardwood floors but the dust is grittier.

Vinyl tile and linoleum flooring are not as dirty or odorous, but usually no one is allowed to walk on the surface for at least 24 hours. You would be well-advised to schedule flooring work for a time when you can move out temporarily.

If workers will still be on site after these tasks are completed, be certain that the floors are carefully protected with rosin paper or tarps. If tarps are used, make sure they are clean ones. (Bits of concrete or plaster that fall from a tarp can leave the first marks on your new floor.)

Your Greatest Contribution Now Is to Be Available

Perhaps at no other stage of construction is the homeowner more needed than now. Towel bars have to be placed, knob locations need to be chosen, and the site for decorative tiles must be selected. Let the contractor know when you'll be available to consult with the workers, and then be certain that you are there so that their work is not delayed.

When they do need you, be decisive. If need be, invite your mother, your decorator, or your friend on the day those decisions have to be made. Be prepared to provide answers! And don't expect the worker to put forth much of an opinion. While he may have excellent comments on how to make something work better, resist asking, "Do you think it looks nice there?" Artistic sensibility isn't their job.

This is also the time when deliveries of items such as cabinets and appliances are being made. Take time to examine them. If an appliance

---

Remember the Power of the Word "Stop!"

Sometimes you'll encounter a problem in home renovation where you really don't know what to do. First, talk to the contractor and try to solve the problem then and there. If you're still not satisfied (or the contractor or the foreman aren't there), ask the workers to stop temporarily. You can suggest they work on something else or take an early lunch until you resolve what's bothering you. Sometimes you just need time.

One homeowner had provided a special molding to go around her tin ceiling. As they were installing it, it looked too big. "No one was on site to talk to, and since my husband had helped me pick it out, I really wanted him to take a look at it. I was beside myself, but I finally asked the workers to quit for the day."

Within 24 hours, husband, wife, and contractor agreed that it was the wrong molding. New molding was ordered, and the delay cost the homeowner an additional $400: "It was worth it. If they had fully installed it, I would have paid more to have it removed, and since I wasn't happy with the look, I certainly didn't want to have to live with it."

---

looks funny, have someone take a look at it immediately. If there is a problem, the sooner it's discovered, the less delay there will be.

Examine the finish materials as they arrive. Look for uniformity of materials in products like tile or brickwork. Or, if you handpicked the marble slabs that are being used, be certain they are the ones you selected and that they match.

If any work phase is particularly critical, make an effort to be home when the workers are getting organized. One homeowner carefully planned out a diamond floor design for his front hallway. When he arrived home, the workers had put it down "checkerboard-style." "I should have been there," the homeowner said ruefully.

Something Major Isn't Right

You know the feeling. Every time you look at something, you get a heavy feeling in the pit of your stomach . . . "How could I have invested all this time and all this money, and it isn't the way I wanted it . . . ?"

It happens. Here's what to do:

- Don't settle—yet. It is your project, and if you and the contractor have worked well together everyone wants you to be satisfied.

- Open a discussion on the topic with the contractor, and tell him what's bothering you. Unless the problem has to do with a finishing detail that has just become apparent, you'd be well advised to comment on the fact that you wish you had realized the problem earlier. This at least puts the contractor into a good frame of mind to hear you out. He wants to please you, but he also is trying hard to finish up.

- Listen carefully to the contractor's response. There may be a good reason for the way it looks. You may think they cut the door too short, but it may actually provide for ventilation and for expansion during periods of high humidity.

  One homeowner actually won an aesthetic battle over something, but regretted his victory later. The fellow couldn't stand the look of leaders and gutters on the house and would not permit the contractor to install them. One night there was a torrential downpour, and the homeowner was shocked to awaken to find his basement flooded. Had he had gutters and leaders to distribute the water and direct it away from his foundation walls, the flooding wouldn't have occurred. Only after this experience did he concede that they were ugly—but practical.

- Be open to suggestion. Perhaps there is a compromise solution. This sometimes happens with on-the-job damage. As mentioned in the previous chapter, countless new bathtubs are damaged before construction is completed because they weren't well pro-

---

CONTRACTOR TIP

Keep It Rolling

The best "finishes" we've experienced are ones in which the job takes on a life of its own. There are no big obstacles and no major delays. Any homeowner-provided materials are on site and have been deemed satisfactory, and the job just keeps on rolling.

Some jobs break down at every turn and seem like they'll never end, but anything you can do to see that your job keeps moving will pay off with a faster finish. From telling the men "good work" to maintain their enthusiasm for the job to being certain that everything you've promised is on hand, anything you can do to make the job go smoothly will hasten the day you'll be able to say a cheerful good-bye to the crew.

Fingerprints and Crooked Light Switch Plates

"How can he come in here with dirty hands!" is the homeowner's frequent lament. The electrician comes from his previous job where they're roughing in the wiring on a house, and he arrives with orders to install your ceiling fixtures. You know the rest. Right up there by the fixture, on the freshly painted ceiling, is a handprint.

This is one area in which you can afford to be a pleasant nag. Remind the contractor to tell the workers that you're in the final stages of the job, so "would they please wash their hands before starting work?"

The light switches are also problematic. Don't let the electricians set the switch plates by eye. Tell your contractor you want him or her to use a torpedo level for setting the plates. This will serve two purposes: It will let them know you're serious about having the switch plates placed correctly, and if they don't actually use the level you've requested, they will know that you'll be calling them back to reset the switch if it isn't right.

tected once in place. Though legally the contractor owes the homeowner a new tub, it usually is the homeowner who starts asking about cosmetic repairs; the thought of breaking out the newly-set tub and turning the house upside down again is more than a homeowner can bear. (As advised previously, protect your tub so you don't have to compromise!)

- Ask if whatever is bothering you can be rebuilt. Who pays depends on where the mistake lies. One client couldn't envision anything on paper. The architect asked the contractor to build and tear down six different versions of the addition so that the homeowner could actually see what each variation would look like. This happened six times, at the owner's expense, before the contractor finally left the job because he couldn't keep his business going with one crew permanently occupied at the same house. In cases where the contractor and his crew have made the error, the contractor will pay to rectify it.
- If there's something you don't like, don't get crazy. (Too many people yell at this stage.) Start with the philosophy that these things happen and that it can be worked out. If you're working with an honorable contractor, he'll make good.

A Well-Timed Walk-Through

When the job is about 95% complete, walk through it with the contractor or the job foreman. This provides an opportunity to see what still needs to be done and to make any decisions that need to be made at this time.

During your walk-through, you may notice things that bother you. This is the beginning of what will be a homeowner-contractor discussion. Certain items will correctable, and others won't, so you'll have to decide what you can live with. One resource you might find helpful during these discussions is a book put out by the National Association of Home Builders called *Quality Standards for the Professional Remodeler*, because it establishes recommended standards of workmanship (See the resource section.) It can be used to negotiate difficulties. If your custom-built bookshelves don't fit snugly against the wall, and the contractor wants to disguise the gap with molding, check the manual: "Gaps in excess of one-quarter inch are unacceptable." It also specifies corrective action: "The remodeler should reposition or reinstall the cabinets." Contractors aren't bound to accept this, but it certainly provides you with information that can be helpful in a negotiation.

Contractors are usually sympathetic to the obviously flawed but less so to the difficult-to-find. If a homeowner has to stand on a ladder and shine a flashlight to display the imperfection of a couple of tiles, he loses a lot of credibility. After all, who is going to notice that? Start your

---

HOMEOWNER TIP

Hire Your Painter Carefully

This is not the time to "settle" for any old painter. A lot of effort has gone into remodeling, and the paint job should do it justice.

Find your painter through referrals, and get references that you check. See at least one home where the crew has worked. You're looking for quality painting, but look, too, for careful workmanship. A not-so-good painter left scratches on six French doors and two sets of sidelights in our house by using a heavy hand with a razor blade when he scraped away the paint he'd spattered on the brand new glass windows. (Like the person who settles for a cosmetic repair on her brand new, now-chipped tub, this was when we finally had to say, "Nothing is perfect.")

list of problems to be resolved, but save your urgent pleas for those that you can't live with.

If your appliances are in place, ask if they are properly hooked up and run them—preferably while the plumber is still on the job. That way you can ask questions or get problems fixed.

As you begin to use new items, watch for leaks. You don't want to believe that the new bathtub you put in above the front hall could produce a wet spot in the hall ceiling but the sooner you notice it, the easier it will be to fix.

Choose Your Paint Colors!

If you have not yet made your final selection of paint, there's no more time for delay. Settle on the colors you want now so that you'll have them for the painter or the contractor before they are needed. On more than one occasion, painter and homeowner (or painter, homeowner, and contractor) have stood around while the decorator or the homeowner selects the exact shade for a room. Then there's more down time while the head painter leaves to buy it. This just costs more time.

When making your selections, don't rely on the color strip for your final selection. Purchase a small quantity of all colors you plan to use. Apply the paint (and any others you're considering) in several areas of the room where it is to be used. This allows you see the color at various times of the day and in various lights to make certain you're pleased with it.

Cleanup

Basic cleanup generally occurs before the painters arrive. Whatever was specified in your contract is what you can expect: "broom clean" is generally specified for the inside, and "rough grade in need of topsoil, landscaping, and seeding" for the outside.

Although you may want to hire a cleaning crew for some help, most homeowners find they can't wait to get it clean themselves—after having so many people in the house, it's actually pleasant to exert this ultimate control.

Finding a Painter

Painting is a time-consuming process, and many contractors do not include it as part of the job. If you need to hire the painter separately, near the end of the finish phase is a good time to do so. The work is close enough to being completed that painters can give you an accurate bid on the job, and with luck, the contractor will be able to provide you with a date when his crew will be gone.

Just as you shouldn't hire a contractor who is not licensed or bonded, the same is true for a painter. When Dan Stone moved to Easthampton, New York, the old home he purchased needed a lot of painting. "I hired a fellow who was working around the neighborhood," says Dan. "He had no license or credentials other than having painted 'a few houses.' Well, I'd never owned a home, and I figured, 'how bad could he be?'"

"First of all, it took them months to do the work. They weren't terrible painters but they kept an erratic schedule and were disorganized. They also convinced me to let them do a special floor stain. They were there the day we pulled up with the moving van, and so I was able to personally ask them "WHY isn't the floor dry?"

"No problem," the painter said. "It's just a little tacky. Everybody knows you can put down butcher paper on a wet floor, and it will come right up later. . . ."

So that's what we did.

Dan continues: "It's three years later now. Do I need to tell you that just yesterday I was picking at some more of the scraps of butcher paper that never came up?"

If you've liked your contractor, then your best source for recommendations on painters is right there in your own house. Chances are your contractor has several names to give you. You can also get recommendations from friends. Call three or four painters to give you estimates. Talk price and calendar. What's it going to cost (and for what prep work and how many coats)? Will he be able to fit you in about the time when your house will be ready?

And check references. Ask these questions:

- Were the painters easy to have around? ("Pleasant" is more important than ever now!)
- Were they neat and careful about built-ins and floor surfaces?
- Did they show up when they were supposed to?

Once you decide on the painter you want to use, spell out responsibilities. There will be some gray areas between where the contractor's job ends and the painter's job begins, so talk to both parties to make certain everyone agrees on who does what. One gray area in renovation concerns nail holes. Generally, it's best to specify that the painters fill nail holes after the prime coat of paint and do any caulking before the finish coat.

Painting

When the painters arrive, show them where they are to set up and in what sink they can wash their brushes. If you had a portable toilet, it's

---

CONTRACTOR TIP

Avoid the Dispatcher Syndrome

Toward the end of this stage, the contractor and the crew are not onsite all the time, and things happen while we're not there. This is when the "Dispatcher Syndrome" comes into play.

The homeowner's brand new faucet is dripping, so instead of simply calling the contractor and asking that it be taken care of (a perfectly reasonable request), Mrs. Smith calls the contractor, the job foreman, the plumber, the electrician (go figure), and last but not least, the architect, "My faucet is dripping, and there's no one here to fix it!"

Had I come back to my office and had just one phone call from Mrs. Smith to return, it would have been much easier to get someone over to work on her faucet. Instead,

I return to my office with calls to respond to from the foreman: "Hey, Mrs. Smith says her faucet is dripping."

From the plumber: "I just heard Mrs. Smith's faucet is dripping. Can't be there until later tonight."

The electrician: "Why would I want to know that Mrs. Smith's faucet is dripping?"

And finally, the architect: "MRS. SMITH'S FAUCET IS DRIPPING!"

So now I have to return all of these phone calls, instead of investigating what's really bothering me—why Mrs. Smith's roof isn't completed yet.

When you first have a problem, make just one phone call. Give us a chance to fix it for you before getting everyone involved.

---

probably gone now, so specify which bathroom they are to use and set any rules you have regarding smoking or use of the telephone.

Communicate instructions to the painters through the head painter. Request extreme care in protecting all surfaces, and insist on clean drop cloths. Point out the newness of everything and ask that they take proper precautions to keep the edges of their ladders from leaving marks on the walls or the floors.

The painter's job is a painstakingly slow one. Wood has to be sanded, walls have to be prepped, and the work has to be done carefully. Prepare for the fact that these workers will be with you for a time.

The painting stage may be interrupted briefly for some work on the Sheetrock. Until the first coat of paint is on, it's difficult to see if the "rockers" have completely sanded away the "holidays." (This expression derives from the thought that the Sheetrocker took a holiday while sanding the finish coat.) Generally, the contractor will pay the painter to correct these flaws.

Homeowner Checklist

- Discuss with your contractor the applications of floor finishes that necessitate your staying elsewhere for a few days. Come up with a mutually agreeable schedule.
- Be sure new floors are protected with rosin paper or clean tarps.
- Be available to make decisions.
- Check deliveries of items such as appliances. Do they seem to be in good condition and are they what was ordered?
- Make sure that materials such as brick and tile are uniform and of the quality you selected.
- Notify the contractor of problems as early as possible, and start with the philosophy that it can all be worked out.
- Mention to the contractor the importance of the finish workers having clean hands.
- If it is not part of your arrangement with the contractor, select your painter.

Chapter 12

→ The Final Good-Bye

"The hardest part of any job is the last nail," say contractors, and by this time the homeowner is eagerly awaiting the last tap of the hammer.

It's almost over, and emotions are high. The contractor and his crew have known all along that after "living with" this family they'd be moving on; the homeowner has prepared for a disrupted life of a certain duration. Now it's time to be finished.

"I couldn't wait to get my house back," says a Virginia homeowner. "We'd remodeled the kitchen, and I was really tired of eating out, bringing in food, or coping with using a microwave to fix dinner in our living room."

"Much as I wanted them out of my house, we'd become friends, and I knew I would miss them," says a homeowner in Los Angeles. "I have little kids, and our afternoons were never boring because we always had nice people to chat with. I knew I'd miss that. I was also angry though. As the job in my home was winding down, they were starting to set up at their next job, and I'd hear them talking about it. I felt like saying, 'Finish this job completely before you start talking about the next one!'"

Mixed emotions or not, your renovation is drawing to a close. It's on to the next job for the contractor, and you're going to get your life back!

But wait. The living room built-ins still have no knobs . . . the new bedroom door squeaks when you open it . . . the electrician never delivered the last light fixture . . . And that's why there's a "punch list."

The Punch List

The "punch list" is your list of "to do" items that need to be finished to make this job complete.

Shortly after your last walk-through with the contractor, you should begin to make your list. Take several days to work on it, and take several strolls through the remodeled part of the house looking for those items that you feel are punch list items. Write everything down.

When the contractor receives your list, he may debate a few of the items. You'll need to negotiate what you can live with and what you can't. In addition, certain elements may simply be "unfixable." One homeowner was displeased with the color of the concrete around his pool house. The contractor reminded him that the day the concrete was to be poured, the temperature was hovering around 100 degrees and he had recommended a delay. The homeowner insisted that it be poured anyway, so to keep the concrete cool enough to pour the crew had to keep wetting it down. As a result, it dried in several gradations of grey. Of course, no one, not even the displeased homeowner, was prepared to tear out all the concrete.

Sometimes items that had nothing to do with the job show up on the punch list. If your kitchen was being remodeled, it is highly unlikely that this is the reason your bedroom window sticks. Certain items veer into the "handyman" category and, although your contractor may be more than happy to help you out, it's not a punch list item. You'll need to pay separately for the work, and it would be unfair to hold back any of the final payment for the overall job until that problem is fixed.

After the punch list has been agreed upon, the contractor will gather what is needed for supplies. Some items may not be easy to locate, so it may take a week or so before someone comes back to take care of the details.

Request that your punch list be taken care of on a specific day or two (or longer for a larger job). There's nothing more annoying than having a worker run in for 30 minutes one day and then tell you he'll "probably be back tomorrow sometime . . ."

Dealing with Damage

That scratch on the new oak floor in the hallway . . . The leg that came off the old table when they moved it back into place . . . The blinds they must have thrown out . . . The nick in the cabinet that must have occurred during installation . . . There will always be damage.

One of the problems with damage is that often it's difficult to point the finger . . . Did the scratch on the floor come from a worker or did it happen when your son brought his skateboard inside? No one will ever be sure. And the worst of it is, the worker may have caused the first scratch, but tomorrow your son's Rollerblades may well add some "character" to the floor as well. Of course, you'll want to negotiate. But do so fairly. If the contractor gave you your money's worth (and perhaps more), he probably deserves better than to have to discuss a $20 item here and a $35 item there. If, however, the workers were negligent and didn't protect your surfaces, then you need to have a serious discussion that determines what he'll pay for or replace.

Remember It's One List—Not Lists

"The Case of the Multiplying Lists" is a tale that is told at the conclusion of more jobs than we would like.

The homeowner and I will go through the job site, marking items we both see that need to be fixed or finished. We'll agree on the list, and my staff will spend three days gathering everything we need in order to finish up. Often the items are hard-to-find finishing touches that require connections and sleuthing in order to find exactly what is needed. The gathering is a time-consuming business. What's more, we don't like to send a worker who is going to spend the day dodging in and out whenever he needs an extra nail.

So my worker arrives in the morning with a hardware-store bag full of supplies, his tools, his schedule of which subcontractor arrives at what time, his lunch, and his list. The homeowner greets him at the door with a long list of "additional items."

This isn't good business. You're tired of having us there, and we're tired of being there. That's why it's so important that the homeowner give careful thought to putting together a single punch list. Present the contractor with that one list, and let him do the job right.

Anything that comes to light afterward falls into the warranty category (see below) or is a handyman task. It can be taken care of but not as part of the punch list.

Settling Up

Once the punch list has been completed, it's time for the final payment. The contractor has earned it, so pay promptly. A letter of thanks isn't a bad idea either. You might like preferential treatment when you call the contractor to take a look at a few of the items under warranty.

Sometimes a couple of punch-list items become bones of contention. You may just hate the bump in the bedroom floor where the old house meets the new, but they simply haven't been able to resolve it to your satisfaction. And broken outlet covers and faulty door knobs are the types of items that linger on and on—big enough to be a real eyesore, but too small for some contractors to want to deal with when he is ready to move on to the next job.

We recommend that you and the contractor discuss what it will cost to have someone else come in to take care of the remainder of the punch-list items. Agree on a mutually acceptable figure.

Give the contractor the bulk of his final payment, holding back three times the amount you've agreed upon.

Now you have more than ample funds to hire someone else to complete the task, and the contractor (who was evidently unable to take care of it to your satisfaction) can go on about his business.

Warranties

Although items such as a furnace or an air-conditioning system will be under warranty from the manufacturer, contractors should also warranty their work—most do so for a year. It can take that long for certain problems (such as the effect of the house settling) to become evident. A few of the things you may notice as the house settles are:

- As the wood in the framing settles, it shrinks and nails pop through the Sheetrock. You may want these repaired.
- Caulking shrinks over time, so you may want someone to come back and grout and caulk once shrinkage has occurred.
- Leaks, particularly around skylights.
- The backfill around the foundation may settle too much. (The land should slope away from the house.) If it seems to be leveling off, talk to the contractor about adding fill.

There may be other things that bother you, and you can consult with your contractor about their repair.

INSIDER'S TIP

What You Should Have when They Leave

- Ask for demonstrations of everything from window locks to how the air-conditioner filters are cleaned. Make sure you understand how things work before they leave.
- Particularly if your electrical system has been upgraded, ask if they can put new labels in the breaker box stating which circuits go to which rooms. This will be invaluable for years to come.

- Be sure the contractor leaves you with the following items:
  - New certificate of occupancy, indicating that your home has been fully inspected and meets all local building requirements. (Don't make your final payment until you have this.)
  - Copies of product warranties and instructions.
  - Telephone numbers of the tradesmen you liked.

Getting to Know Your New House

Your house is different now—not just in having a larger kitchen or a new bathroom with a skylight—there are going to be other changes too, and it's going to take time to get to know the new place. Air may circulate differently, the water pressure may be stronger (or the temperature hotter), the new gutters and leaders may make different noises when it rains.

Part of the adventure of home renovation is learning what those new squeaks mean, and experimenting as to what to do when you notice that the attic fan isn't drawing the way it used to. For some items you may need to call the contractor to ask questions, in other cases you will call the specialist involved directly (these people will be added to your telephone directory).

As you begin to settle in, you'll soon find that your newly renovated home is as bright and spacious and beautiful as you'd dreamed. It was worth the dust, the interminable comings and goings of the crew, and the constant concern over whether the project would ultimately be "right."

In a post-job call to the contractor, one homeowner said it best: "I knew it was going to be nice, but I didn't know it was going to be this nice. Thank you!"

Homeowner Checklist

- Take several days to create one thorough punch list for your contractor.
- Request that the contractor assign someone to work on your punch list items during a specific block of time (several days? a week?). You do not want it taken care of piecemeal.
- Be certain the contractor leaves you with these items:
  - new certificate of occupancy
  - product warranties and instructions
  - telephone numbers of the tradespeople whom you liked
- After making any agreed-upon deductions for damage or unfinished punch-list items, give the contractor his final payment.

▸ Reading Blueprints

Many people take the time and go through the expense of working with an architect, only to get the plans and never give them more than a cursory look. The attitude is, "Well, of course, they're okay. They were drawn by a professional!"

Yes, they were, but that still doesn't mean that they are perfect or that every detail that matters to you has been spelled out. That's why it's absolutely vital that you read your blueprints and understand what they mean.

In general, blueprints consist of three views of your home:

The Site or Floor Plan. This view is the one that looks straight down on the project. An exterior view of your house showing the footprint (the space your house takes up) of your home is a site plan. An interior view is a floor plan.

An Elevation. This is a straight-on view that shows exactly what your house looks like from either the exterior or the interior. Interior elevations might show the details of a fireplace, or how high the bathroom tile is to be placed.

A Section. This view details a "slice" of something. If an architect wants to show a contractor how a wall or a cabinet is to be constructed, he does so by drawing a section.

Floor plans are usually in $1/4$-inch scale, elevations and details (an enlargement of a particular item, such as a window detail) are usually in $1/2$-inch scale or larger.

In addition to these renderings, you'll find numerous details throughout your plans. Read them all. Some of the notations will refer to specific items that are pictured. Others will be in the form of "schedules" such as a "door schedule," a "window schedule," or a "finish schedule." These schedules list all the items necessary for that particular job.

Your specs for the jobs—all the detailed instructions concerning what goes in, where, and how—may be incorporated in your blueprints. Generally, if the specs are on the blueprints, they run down one side of each page. Sometimes, however, the specs come as a separate document.

Your contract, your blueprints, and your specifications are all important documents, and you'll want two sets of each. One set, the set that all parties involved have signed and initialed, should be placed in your safe deposit box for safekeeping. Should anything go wrong with the project, this is your legal protection. The other set becomes your working document, and the set you'll refer to throughout the project.

What follows is a guide to blueprints. However, if there is something you still don't understand about yours, ask your architect or design professional. They'll be happy to explain them to you.

GRAPHIC MATERIAL SYMBOLS

These symbols are some of the abstract conventions commonly used in architectural construction drawings.

EARTH	earth	rock	gravel fill	
CONCRETE	structural	lightweight	block	block
BRICK	common brick	face brick	fire brick	plaster, sand, cement grout
STONE	cut stone	rubble	cast stone	marble / slate
METAL	iron/steel	aluminum	brass/bronze	sheet metal/all metals at small scale / structural
WOOD	finish	rough	plywood (large scale)	plywood (small scale) / wood stud walls
INSULATION	loose or batt	rigid	rigid insulation	small scale / STRUCTURAL CLAY TILE
MISCELLANEOUS	resilient flooring	acoustical tile	waterproofing/flashing	glass (large scale) / glass (small scale)

• PLAN AND SECTION INDICATIONS

GLAZING				
CONCRETE/PLASTER		STONE	ashlar	rubble
MASONRY	brick	block	running bond	stack bond / ceramic tile
WOOD	shingles	panel		
METAL	metal			

• ELEVATION INDICATIONS

Within the limitations of the scale of the drawing, a material's scale, texture, and pattern should be drawn as accurately as possible.

SITE PLAN

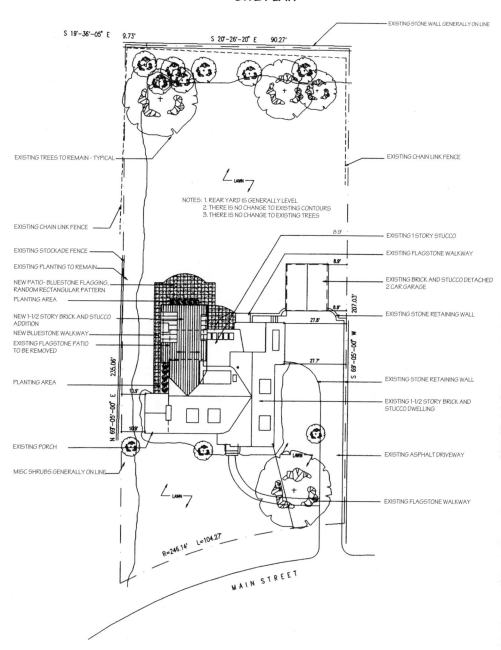

S 19'-36'-05" E   9.73'

S 20'-26'-20" E   90.27'

EXISTING STONE WALL GENERALLY ON LINE

EXISTING TREES TO REMAIN - TYPICAL

EXISTING CHAIN LINK FENCE

LAWN

NOTES: 1. REAR YARD IS GENERALLY LEVEL
2. THERE IS NO CHANGE TO EXISTING CONTOURS
3. THERE IS NO CHANGE TO EXISTING TREES

EXISTING CHAIN LINK FENCE

8.9'

EXISTING 1 STORY STUCCO

EXISTING STOCKADE FENCE

EXISTING FLAGSTONE WALKWAY

EXISTING PLANTING TO REMAIN

8.8'

NEW PATIO- BLUESTONE FLAGGING,
RANDOM RECTANGULAR PATTERN

EXISTING BRICK AND STUCCO DETACHED
2 CAR GARAGE

PLANTING AREA

8.9'

207.03'

NEW 1-1/2 STORY BRICK AND STUCCO
ADDITION

27.8'

EXISTING STONE RETAINING WALL

NEW BLUESTONE WALKWAY

EXISTING FLAGSTONE PATIO
TO BE REMOVED

27.7'

235.06'

PLANTING AREA

EXISTING STONE RETAINING WALL

10.9'

S 69'-05'-00" W

EXISTING 1-1/2 STORY BRICK AND
STUCCO DWELLING

N 69'-05'-00" E

10.9'

EXISTING PORCH

MISC SHRUBS GENERALLY ON LINE

EXISTING ASPHALT DRIVEWAY

LAWN

EXISTING FLAGSTONE WALKWAY

LAWN

R=246.14'   L=104.27'

MAIN STREET

UPSTAIRS FLOOR PLAN

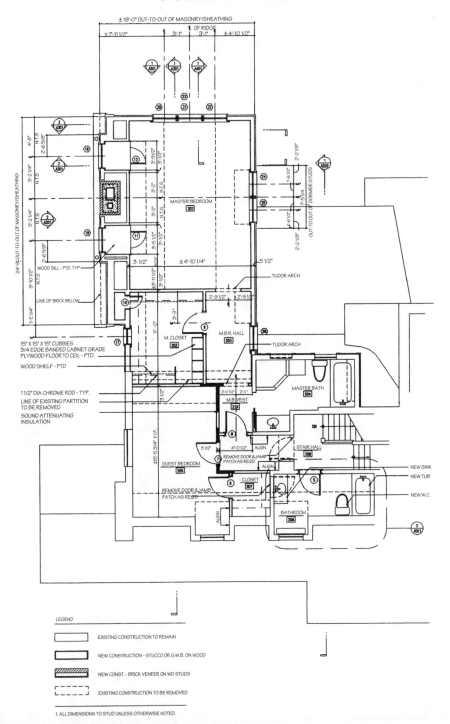

LEGEND

EXISTING CONSTRUCTION TO REMAIN

NEW CONSTRUCTION - STUCCO OR G.W.B. ON WOOD

NEW CONST. - BRICK VENEER ON WD STUDS

EXISTING CONSTRUCTION TO BE REMOVED

1. ALL DIMENSIONS TO STUD UNLESS OTHERWISE NOTED.

REAR ELEVATION

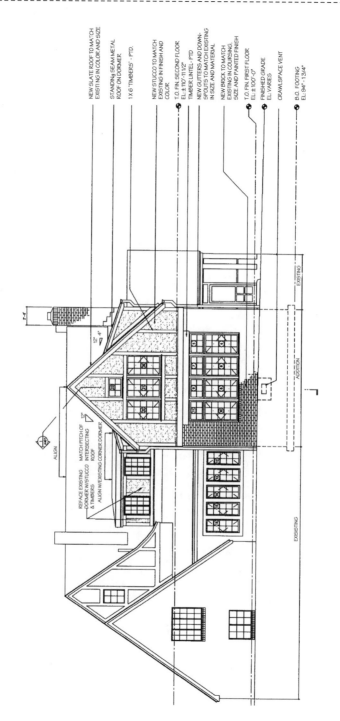

NEW SLATE ROOF TO MATCH EXISTING IN COLOR AND SIZE

STANDING SEAM METAL ROOF ON DORMER

1 X 6 "TIMBERS" - PTD.

NEW STUCCO TO MATCH EXISTING IN FINISH AND COLOR

T.O. FIN. SECOND FLOOR
EL ± 110'-11 1/2"

TIMBER LINTEL - PTD

NEW GUTTERS AND DOWN-SPOUTS TO MATCH EXISTING IN SIZE AND MATERIAL

NEW BRICK TO MATCH EXISTING IN COURSING, SIZE, AND PAINTED FINISH

T.O. FIN. FIRST FLOOR
EL ± 100'-0"

FINISHED GRADE
EL. VARIES

CRAWLSPACE VENT

B.O. FOOTING
EL. 94' - 1 3/4"

REFACE EXISTING DORMER W/STUCCO & TIMBERS

MATCH PITCH OF INTERSECTING ROOF

ALIGN W/EXISTING CORNER DORMER

ALIGN

EXISTING

ADDITION

EXISTING

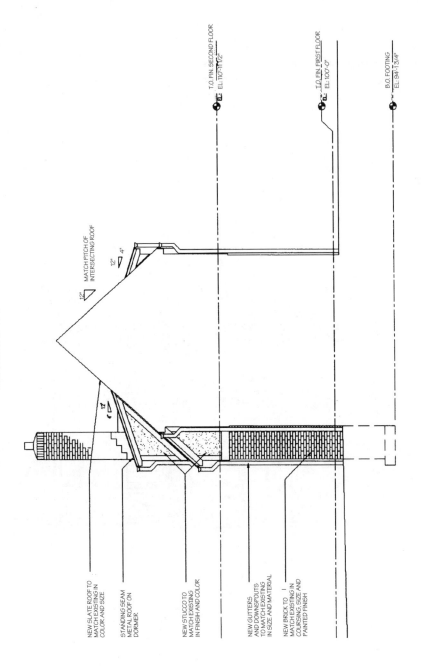

SIDE ELEVATION

MATCH PITCH OF
INTERSECTING ROOF

12"
4"

12"
4"

NEW SLATE ROOF TO
MATCH EXISTING IN
COLOR AND SIZE

STANDING SEAM
METAL ROOF ON
DORMER

NEW STUCCO TO
MATCH EXISTING
IN FINISH AND COLOR

NEW GUTTERS
AND DOWNSPOUTS
TO MATCH EXISTING
IN SIZE AND MATERIAL

NEW BRICK TO
MATCH EXISTING IN
COURSING, SIZE AND
PAINTED FINISH

T.O. FIN. SECOND FLOOR
EL. 110'-11 1/2"

T.O. FIN. FIRST FLOOR
EL. 100'-0"

B.O. FOOTING
EL. 94'-1 3/4"

BUILDING SECTION

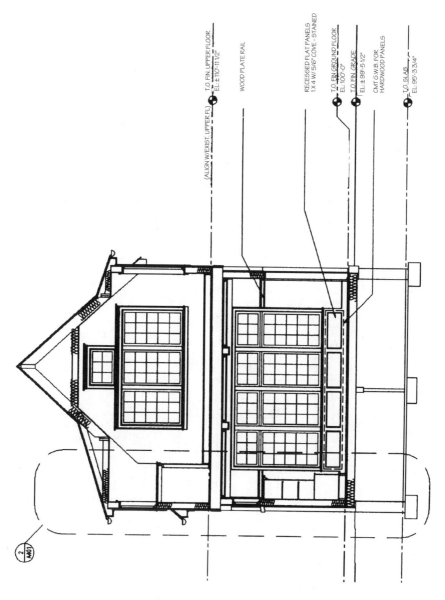

(ALIGN W/ EXIST. UPPER FL) T.O. FIN. UPPER FLOOR
EL. ± 110'-11 1/2"

WOOD PLATE RAIL

RECESSED FLAT PANELS
1 X 4 W/ 5/6" COVE - STAINED

T.O. FIN. GROUND FLOOR
EL. 100'-0"

T.O. FIN. GRADE
EL. ± 99'-5 1/2"

CMT G.W.B. FOR
HARDWOOD PANELS

T.O. SLAB
EL. 95'-3 3/4"

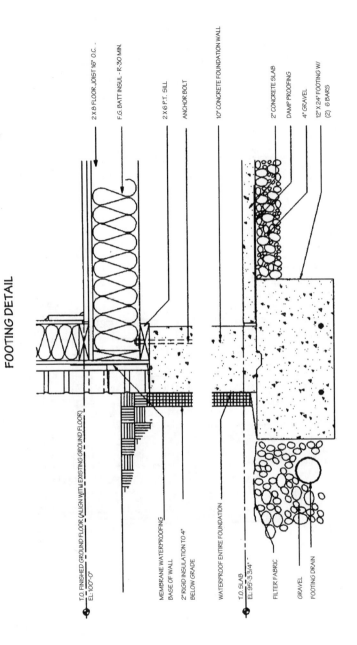

FOOTING DETAIL

2 X 8 FLOOR JOIST 16" O.C.

F.G. BATT INSUL - R-30 MIN.

2 X 6 P.T. SILL

ANCHOR BOLT

10" CONCRETE FOUNDATION WALL

2" CONCRETE SLAB

DAMP PROOFING

4" GRAVEL

12" X 24" FOOTING W/ (2) 6 BARS

T.O. FINISHED GROUND FLOOR (ALIGN WITH EXISTING GROUND FLOOR)
EL. 100'-0"

MEMBRANE WATERPROOFING

BASE OF WALL

2" RIGID INSULATION TO 4"
BELOW GRADE

WATERPROOF ENTIRE FOUNDATION

T.O. SLAB
EL. 95'-3 3/4"

FILTER FABRIC

GRAVEL

FOOTING DRAIN

FAMILY ROOM CABINETS

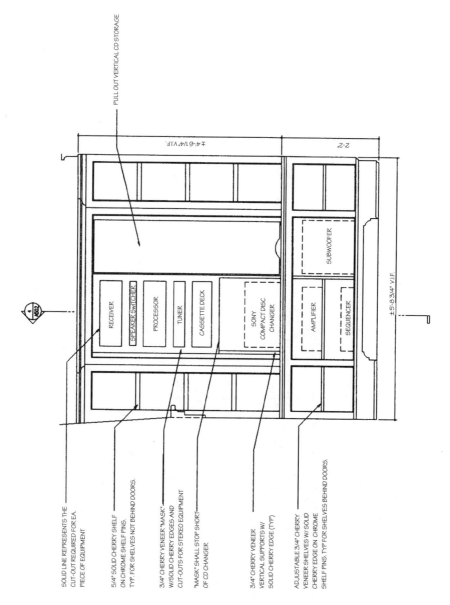

PULL OUT VERTICAL CD STORAGE

±4'-6 1/4" V.I.F.

2'-2"

±5'-8 3/4" V.I.F.

RECEIVER

SPEAKER SWITCHER

PROCESSOR

TUNER

CASSETTE DECK

SONY COMPACT DISC CHANGER

SUBWOOFER

AMPLIFIER

SEQUENCER

SOLID LINE REPRESENTS THE CUT-OUT REQUIRED FOR EA. PIECE OF EQUIPMENT

5/4" SOLID CHERRY SHELF ON CHROME SHELF PINS. TYP. FOR SHELVES NOT BEHIND DOORS.

3/4" CHERRY VENEER "MASK" W/ SOLID CHERRY EDGES AND CUT-OUTS FOR STEREO EQUIPMENT

"MASK" SHALL STOP SHORT OF CD CHANGER

3/4" CHERRY VENEER VERTICAL SUPPORTS W/ SOLID CHERRY EDGE (TYP)

ADJUSTABLE 3/4" CHERRY VENEER SHELVES W/ SOLID CHERRY EDGE ON CHROME SHELF PINS. TYP FOR SHELVES BEHIND DOORS.

DOOR SCHEDULE AND DOOR TYPES

NO	MANUFACTURER	DIMENSION WIDTH	HEIGHT	THICK	TYPE	MATL/FIN	JAMB WIDTH	SILL	CASING	HARDW	REMARKS
											DOOR SCHEDULE
FIRST FLOOR											
1	ENJO	2'-6"	6'-8"	13/4"	A	WOOD/ST.	4 9/16"	-	-	A	
2	ENJO J701	2 @ 2'-6"	6'-8"	13/4"	D	WOOD/ST.	V.I.F	-	-	E	TEMPERED SAFETY GLASS
3	ENJO	2@2'-6"	6'-8"	13/4"	A	WOOD/ST.	V.I.F.	-	-	B	POCKET DOOR-STAN F.R. SIDE/PTD. B.R. SIDE
4	PELLA-AI-26FM	2@3'-0"	6'-8"	13/4"	B	WOOD/ST.	6 9/16"	-	-	C	R.O. WIDTH=6'-2 1/4" R.O. HT=6'-10" -PRIME EXT
5	EXISTING	±2'-6"	±6'-7"	V.I.F.	-	/PTD.	V.I.F.	-	-	O	REUSE EXISTING DOOR @ M.B.R.
6	ENJO	2'-6"	6'-8"	13/4"	A	WOOD/PTD.	6 9/16"	-	-	D	
7	ENJO	2'-6"	6'-8"	13/4"	A	WOOD/PTD	6 9/16"	-	-	A	
8	ENJO	2'-6"	6'-8"	13/4"	A	WOOD/PTD	6 9/16"	-	-	A	
9	ENJO	2'-6"	6'-8"	13/4"	A	WOOD/PTD	6 9/16"	-	-	D	
10	CUSTOM	1'-6"	2'-0"	3/4"	E	WOOD/PTD	6 9/16"	-	-	F	CONCEALED DOOR
11	CUSTOM	2'-8"	3'-0"	3/4"	F	WOOD/PTD	6 9/16"	-	-	G	
12	CUSTOM	2'-8"	3'-0"	3/4"	F	WOOD/PTD	6 9/16"	-	-	G	
13	BROSCO	2@3'-0"	6'-8"	11/16"	C	WOOD/PTD	-	-	-	H	EASY CHANGE ULTRA-VU (PROVIDE ALT FOR PELLA)

ELECTRICAL PLAN OF FAMILY ROOM

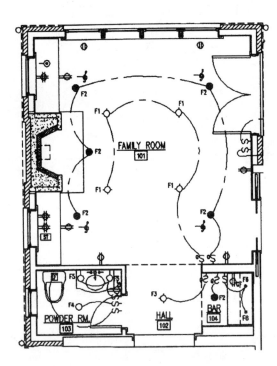

Resources

For information on government loans for home improvement:

> Call 201-676-6639; ask about *The Consumer's Guide to Home Repair Grants and Subsidized Loans.*

For a copy of *Remodeling* magazine's *Cost Value Report*, contact:

> *Remodeling* magazine
> 202-452-0800
> One Thomas Circle NW
> Washington, DC 20005

For a list of architects in your area and a list of sample contracts for home remodeling, contact:

> American Institute of Architects
> 1735 New York Ave. NW
> Washington, DC 20006

For names of kitchen and bath designers and information on planning kitchen and bath space, contact:

> National Kitchen and Bath Association
> 687 Willow Grove St.
> Hackettstown, NJ 07840

For names of designers in your area, contact:

> American Society of Interior Designers
> 608 Massachusetts Ave. NE
> Washington, DC 20002

Some designers will provide interior decorating only; when you talk to them, clarify that you need someone to help plan remodeling work as well.

Of the computer programs available, the best and most complete at the time this book was written was *3D Home Architect* by Broderbund. It is also recommended by contractors as one that produces serviceable plans.

For referrals to home contractors, contact:

> National Association of the Remodeling Industry
> 4301 N. Fairfax, Suite 310
> Arlington, VA 22203

> The National Association of Home Builders Remodelers Council
> 1201 15th St. NW
> Washington, DC 20009

The NAHB also has publications on the subject, including the book referred to in chapter 11: *Quality Standards for the Professional Remodeler.*

For a list of appropriate publications on remodeling as well as contract information, contact:

The American Homeowners
Foundation
1-800-489-7776
6776 Little Falls Rd.
Arlington, VA 22213-1213

Get more information on lead-based paint from the following sources. For a free brochure:

Call the Center for Disease Control (404) 488-7330 and ask for "Important Facts about Childhood Lead Poisoning Prevention"

National Lead Information Center of the National Safety Council: Call 800-LEADFYI to request brochures.
Call 800-424-LEAD to ask specific questions.

For information on professional lead inspection and removal and a list of approved materials that can be used to cover painted surfaces contact:

National Alliance for Encapsulation
Technology
34 S. Market St.
Frederick, MD 21701

For additional information on abatement contact:

National Lead Abatement Council
Box 535
Olney, MD 20832

For a copy of *Renovating Your Home Without Lead Poisoning Your Children,* send $1 to:

The Conservation Law Foundation
62 Summer St.
Boston, MA 02110

Other booklets on lead are available from the National Safety Council. Call (202) 293-2270.

Glossary

Ampere (Amps): The measurement of the rate of flow of electricity.

Appraiser: A person who determines the value of real estate. Not all states require appraisers to meet stringent licensing requirements.

Backsplash: A protective panel on the wall behind a sink or counter.

Baseboard Trim: A decorative trim placed around the perimeter of interior walls. Used where floor meets wall to create a more finished, attractive appearance.

Bid Breakdown: Rather than give you a lump-sum figure for your remodeling project, contractors break an estimate down into bid phases that describe the work to be performed. Examples include plumbing, heating, electrical, roofing, and all other forms of home construction.

Blueprints: The common name for working plans printed in blue ink that show all aspects of the construction methods to be used in building and remodeling.

Builder-Grade: A trade term that designates a product of average quality.

Casement Window: A window with hinges and a mechanical crank to open and close it. These windows open outward.

Caulking: A mixture used to fill cracks.

Cabinets (Custom): Cabinets that are made one kitchen at a time to the specifications of a particular customer.

Cabinets (Stock): Cabinets produced in quantity and offered in a range of sizes; they can be ordered for a specific kitchen but are not custom made.

Certificate of Occupancy: These are issued by the local codes enforcement office when all building code requirements are met. They allow the legal habitation of a dwelling, and the homeowner would be unable to sell his home without a valid C.O.

Chair Rail: A finished wood trim that is placed horizontally along the wall where chairs might come in contact. A chair rail serves a practical purpose if a chair is likely to be pushed back into the wall regularly (as someone leaves a kitchen table, for example), but it is most frequently used as a decorative trim, usually in kitchens and dining rooms.

Change Order: A written agreement allowing a change from previously agreed-to plans. Change orders detail the nature of the change and all pertinent facts affected by the change. Some cover unexpected items such as the replacement of a worn pipe that was discovered when the walls were opened, others are used in situations when the homeowner decides he wants an extra closet, for instance. With extras, always ask "how much?" Moving a door four inches to the right may cost you $800.

Circuit Breaker: These devices provide protection from an overloaded electrical circuit by shutting down the circuit if it is producing a dangerously heavy electrical current. It is the modern equivalent of an electrical fuse.

Crawl Space: The space beneath a house, between the first story floor joists and the ground. It can also refer to an attic where there is work space but the ceiling is too low to stand up.

Crown Molding: A decorative wood trim placed at the top of an inside wall where the wall meets the ceiling.

Decking: Materials used to build interior floor systems or an exterior deck.

Dedicated Outlet: An electrical outlet on a separate circuit that services one major appliance or device such as a computer.

Demo Work: Demolition; the process of dismantling or destroying existing conditions.

Detail: On a blueprint, this term refers to an enlargement of a particular architectural item such as the design of a window.

Elevations: Refers to illustrations on the blueprints, specifically picture drawings of the front of a house, the side of the house, and the rear of the house. There can also be elevations of an interior detail such as a fireplace.

Exterior Framing: The material or labor used in constructing exterior walls and roof structures.

Fiberboard: A composite sheet made from pressed materials bonded together for use as a wall sheathing.

Fire-stop: A fire-stop can be made of several substances; its purpose is to block dead air space thereby slowing or preventing fire from traveling from floor to floor or from room to room.

Fitting: Any device that controls water entering or leaving a fixture.

Fixture: A light, such as a ceiling fixture, or a bathtub, shower, lavatory, toilet, bidet, or urinal that receives water.

Flashing: Continuous metal protection that directs water away from water-collecting areas, for example, the top of windows or chimneys.

Floor Joist: A board used to support the floor of a house. Floor joists span foundation walls at regular intervals to provide strength and support to the finished floor.

Footing: A support, usually concrete, under a foundation that provides a larger base than the foundation to distribute weight. The footing reduces settling and shifting foundations.

Foundation: The base of a structure used to support the entire structure.

Framing: A trade term that refers to the process of building the frame structure of a home and applies to siding, sheathing, and wall coverings.

Ground Fault Circuit Interrupter (GFCI): A safety component of outlets near a water source. If there is an electrical short, then the GFCI instantly cuts off power to the outlet.

Grout: Substance used to fill cracks between tile during installation of the tile.

HVAC: Heating, ventilation, air conditioning.

In the Field: A term referring to the job site (as opposed to the office).

Interior Trim: Any decorative wood trim used within the home: baseboards, window casing, chair rails, crown molding, and door casings.

Joint Compound: Also referred to as drywall mud, it is used to hide seams and nail or screw heads in a home's finished walls.

Joists: Supporting structural beams, usually wood, allowing the support of floors and ceilings.

Lien: This is a legal document placed on the title of a house by a supplier **(materialman's lien)** or a trades-man **(mechanic's lien)** that prevents the homeowner from selling or transferring ownership of this home until the dispute is resolved. They are placed when suppliers and tradespeople have provided supplies or services to the homeowner and have not been paid by the contractor.

Lien Rights: The right of contractors and suppliers to place a lien when services or products are provided but not paid for.

Lien Waiver: These documents are signed by vendors and subcontractors upon payment to acknowledge payment and to release their right to place a lien against the property.

Linear Feet: A unit of measure that determines the distance between two points in a straight line.

Load-Bearing Walls: Interior or exterior walls that carry the load from above down to the foundation.

Material Legend: An area of the blueprints where materials for the project are described in great detail.

Mechanical Systems: Includes plumbing, heating and cooling equipment, fans that provide ventilation, and the water heater.

Mortar: Lime or cement mixture used between bricks, blocks, or stones to hold them in place.

Nonconforming: A house or improvement dissimilar to surrounding properties in age, size, use, or style. The term is sometimes used to indicate that the home does not conform to current zoning ordinances.

Nonstructural Changes: Changes not affecting the structural integrity of a building. Examples include replacing cabinets, putting in new carpet, painting.

Particleboard: A composite of wood chips bonded and pressed together to create a sheet to be used for subflooring or sheathing.

Plumbing Stack: A pipe rising vertically through a building to carry waste and water to the building sewer or to vent plumbing fixtures. It penetrates the roof of the building.

Prime Coat: The coat of paint applied first to prepare the wall for the finish coats. Walls that are primed will produce better results than those that aren't.

PVC Pipe: Poly Vinyl Chloride, a type of plastic pipe used in plumbing. Frequently used for drains and vents and occasionally used for cold water piping.

Rip-Out: Like it sounds, the removal of existing items to allow for installation of new items. It can happen at various stages, such as during installation of new electrical work and in various locations during home remodeling.

Rough-In: Refers to the installation of material prior to enclosing the walls. Plumbing pipes, heating and air-conditioning ducts, and electrical wiring go in at this stage.

Schematic Design: Rough sketches; one of the earliest stages of home design.

Setback Requirement: Local zoning laws regulate the amount of unobstructed space that must exist between properties. The requirements vary from community to community and establish rules for how far a structure must be from the property line. If a homeowner needs to build closer to the property line and can prove good cause, then a variance must be sought from the local zoning board.

Specs or Specifications: A written description of a project, setting out exactly what will be done and what material will be used. Good specs make a difference when getting an accurate bid.

Square Footage: To determine square footage, measure the length and width of the room and multiply those two measurements. If a proposed addition is 20 feet long and 16 feet wide, then the square feet added is 320 square feet.

Square Yardage: Determine the square footage of your space, then divide by 9. This will give you the square yardage figure. For example, if a room contains 90 square feet, it has 10 square yards of space.

Standard-Grade Fixture: A product of average quality, normally found in production-built housing.

Structural Integrity: The strength of a structure to remain in position without fail. You do not want anyone to do anything to your home that will diminish the structural integrity.

Structural Work: Work that involves the structure: putting on an addition; lifting a roof to create a new room; relocating load-bearing walls.

Studs: In homes, studs are usually made from wood and are the vertical supports in a wall. They are placed at regular intervals to provide support and a nailing surface for wall coverings and exterior siding.

Subcontractor: A contractor who works for a general contractor; plumber, electrician, HVAC workers, masons, etc. Often called "subs" for short.

Subfloor: Generally, plywood or particleboard sheets attached to floor joists under the finished floor coverings.

Support Columns: Vertical columns used for structural support, such as the columns found in basements and garages.

Taped Drywall: Drywall that has been hung and taped. The tape is adhered with a joint compound and is designed to hide the seams where sheets of drywall meet.

Template: Generally referring to a pattern for something, such as a guide for cutting a countertop. A designer might suggest you create a template of a kitchen island to see how you feel when something this size inhabits the middle of your kitchen.

Three-Way Switch: A set of two switches that can operate a light from two different locations, such as the top and bottom of the stairs.

Time and Material Basis (T&M): A form of billing for all labor and material supplied with no cap on the billed amount.

Wainscoting: Wood or tile that is installed on the lower portion of a wall, joined by a chair rail, to meet the upper wall, finished with paint or wallpaper.

Tradespeople: Carpenters, plumbers, electricians, and other trained construction professionals.

Waste Pipe: The line that carries away the discharge from any plumbing fixture.

Worker's Compensation Insurance: Insurance that protects workers who are injured while performing their professional duties.

Working Plans: The documents that are designed to provide enough information for the tradespeople to work from.

Work Triangle: The sink, stove, and refrigerator make up the three points of this triangle.